THE

GREAT REVIVAL OF 1800.

BY THE

REV. WILLIAM SPEER, D.D.

PHILADELPHIA:
PRESBYTERIAN BOARD OF PUBLICATION,
No. 1334 CHESTNUT STREET.

Entered according to Act of Congress, in the year 1872, by
THE TRUSTEES OF THE
PRESBYTERIAN BOARD OF PUBLICATION,
In the Office of the Librarian of Congress, at Washington.

WESTCOTT & THOMSON,
Stereotypers and Electrotypers, Philada.

CONTENTS.

CHAPTER VIII.

CHAPTER IX.

CHAPTER X.

CHAPTER XI.

THE GREAT REVIVAL OF 1800.

CHAPTER I.

METHOD OF THE ADVANCES OF CHRIST'S KINGDOM—PREVIOUS REVIVALS.

IT is most evident that the Christian Church is again upon the eve of one of those great impulses in the growth of the Kingdom of God on earth which we commonly entitle a "reformation" or "revival."

The Lord Almighty does not carry forward the growth of that Kingdom by an even and gradual expansion, which would leave it to men to claim the glory of it. It advances like a river, which rarely follows far a right line, which may, for long distances, be troubled and turbid, but suddenly breaks out at intervals upon its course into broad, peaceful expansions or lakes, surrounded by scenes of extraordinary fertility and beauty. It grows upon a principle like that which the Creator has impressed upon many genera of the vegetable kingdom—grasses, canes, trees—by a succession of nodes, or axes, or joints; points where, at considerable distances apart, the compressed life of the stem breaks out into spreading branches, laden with foliage and fruit. The Kingdom of God has thus ever increased by a succession of sudden and vigorous expansions, whose intervals have not been without regularity or plan. It is one of those great expansions of spiritual life which seems now to be at hand.

From the earliest history of the world these periods of revival have been distinguished by the visitation of our race with such judgments as would compel men to think of their fallen, sinful, helpless, perishing condition; of the infinite power and offended justice of God; of the necessity of a propitiation and atonement for sin in such ways as He might offer; and of the duties of repentance, submission, obedience, and preparation for an account before Him. They have been ages of wars, pestilence, earthquakes, sudden and vast changes in social order, signs or discoveries in the heavens. Strange to tell, these judgments have irritated rather than humbled God's enemies, and produced crimes more outrageous, unbelief more determined, and resistance and persecutions of God's most beloved and faithful messengers and servants.

These great expansions have been attended in the arrangements of the Divine Ruler by various and munificent gifts of those agencies of civilization which would facilitate the spread and increase of the spiritual mercies, and enlarge the enjoyment and multiply the benefits of them. They have, therefore, been the world's conspicuous eras of geographical discovery, of wide-spread commerce, of wealth in the precious metals, of useful inventions, of social refinement and polish, of remunerative researches of science, of liberation of thought, and of emancipation of oppressed races.

The colonization of this republic was induced to a remarkable extent by a great quickening in Europe during the seventeenth century, which moved multitudes from its different nations and churches to seek here opportunities for greater freedom and spirituality of faith and worship. It was an age of vast commercial enterprise. It was the era in Great Britain of bloody and protracted civil wars, of dreadful licentiousness and corruption, of the Great Plague and the Great Fire of London, in two consecutive years, 1665 and 1666. During it, sounded forth the seraphic gospel trumpets of Richard Baxter, Philip and Matthew Henry, John Flavel, Alexander Henderson, John Livingstone and others, whose preaching was accompanied by amazing scenes of spiritual power. Such was the revival of the Kirk of Shotts, in which under one sermon five hundred persons were subdued to Christ.

The influence of this period of revival was felt in the feeble colonies of America. Since then there have been several periods specially marked by general revivals of religion. The two which are the most distinguished for the power with which the Holy Spirit was poured out, for the distinctness of the concurrent evidences that the work was from God, and by the beneficent results which followed, were those of 1730 and of 1800, and the years adjacent.

The *first* of these revivals was known in the religious history of the century as "The Great Awakening." It commenced during the age of Queen Anne, "The Augustan age of English literature," and also that of Bolingbroke, Hobbes and many of the bitterest enemies of Christianity, whose planting bore its natural fruit in the general contempt for religion and morality. But so profound and so extensive was the impression communicated to Christianity by this quickening from on high that one of our ablest writers (*Isaac Taylor: Wesley and Methodism*) says: "In fact, that great religious movement has, immediately or remotely, so given an impulse to Christian feeling and profession on all sides that it has come to present itself as the starting-point of our modern religious history."

And this "religious epoch," beyond any other time, was that of the rise of modern missions to heathen nations. The Dutch and Danes and Germans planted the gospel in many Eastern lands. Schultz translated and printed the New and parts of the Old Testament in Hindustani, and the whole Bible and numerous tracts in the Telinga; Ziegenbalg and Grundler did the same for the people of Malabar. King Frederick IV. of Denmark was thoroughly interested in the spread of the gospel through the Danish East Indies, and set apart large funds for this end. The ever-memorable missions of the Moravians commenced then. Christian David and Matthew and Christian Stack set out for their heroic work in Greenland amidst the January snows at Hernhut, in 1733, soon followed by the no less devoted Dober and Nitschman upon their way to preach Christ to the degraded black slaves in the West Indies. And within a few years (1739) Christian Henry Rauch began to preach in their guttural tongue to the Mohegan Indians in New York, and planted the town of Bethlehem, which still remains, in Pennsylvania. The English Society for Promoting Christian Knowledge did much for India and the East. The Scotch Society for Propagating Christian Knowledge supported in this country David and John Brainerd, and afterward aided Dr. E. Wheelock in the Indian school which was the foundation of Dartmouth College.

The population of the American colonies was harassed at that time by wars with the Indians and with France. "A remarkable succession of diseases traversed the provinces, or, confined to a few localities, bore off the children and youth, yet those years were not more remarkable for unexampled mortality than for unbridled merriment." Thus God prepared the way for that revival in the New World of which Jonathan Edwards, Whitfield, William and Gilbert Tennant, David Brainerd, Samuel Davies and others were the most remarkable instruments. Edwards said of it: "It is evident that it is a very great and wonderful and exceedingly glorious work of God. This is certain, that it is a great and wonderful event, a strange revolution, an unexpected, surprising overturning of things, suddenly brought to pass, such as has never been seen in New England, and scarce ever has been heard of in any land." It was estimated that this work, in its progress through the colonies, brought to Christ about one in forty of their whole population—a proportion which would be equal to *one million* of the people at present within the limits of our country.

The *second* general revival in America, which was the first in the United States after their independence, was that which is recognized as "The Great Revival of 1800." To give some detailed and practical account of it is our present object. Its beginnings date from the closing years of the preceding century.

CHAPTER II.

PROVIDENTIAL PREPARATIONS--CIVILIZATION—CHASTISEMENTS.

THE period of the Great Revival of 1800 was a notable one in respect to the advances of civilization. The three voyages of Cook, those of Bougainville, Le Perouse, Krusenstern, Behring and others, had made the most distant nations known to the people of Europe and America as they never were before. In France, Germany, Italy, England and the United States, many wonderful discoveries were made in chemistry, electricity, medicine, mathematics, mechanics and astronomy. It was the period when French infidelity, eagerly accepted over Europe, fruited in the crops of the guillotine, in the abandoned licentiousness and tiger-like cruelty of the people of France, in the wars of Napoleon, which were carried on in three continents and moved the interest of the whole world.

This country was prepared for a universal and profound religious movement by the bloodshed, trials and bereavements of the eight years' war of the Revolution. The conflicting interests and ideas of the different colonies, even after the adoption of the Constitution, made thinking men feel that our republican system was a new and perilous experiment. West of the Allegheny Mountains war with the

the Indian tribes, the frequent massacres of families and burning of the new homes and hard-won harvests of the adventurous settlers, the demoniac acts of barbarism committed by renegade white men living with but outdoing the Indians in such acts, and the almost unrestrained prevalence of crime, kept the inhabitants in a continual state of apprehension. A committee of Congress reported in 1800, in respect to the three States into which it was proposed to divide the North-west Territory, that "in the three western countries there has been but one court having cognizance of crimes in five years; and the immunity which offenders experience attracts, as to an asylum, the most vile and abandoned criminals, and at the same time deters useful and virtuous persons from making settlements in such society. This territory is exposed, as a frontier, to foreign nations, whose agents can find sufficient interest in exciting or fomenting insurrection and discontent, as thereby they can more easily divert a valuable trade in furs from the United States."

Religion and morals were at the lowest ebb they have ever reached in this country. Large numbers of men released from the army, where the religious influences of the day were feebly exerted, carried home with them the vices they had contracted and the infidelity which they imbibed from their French allies. The leading statesmen were generally the disciples of the school of Voltaire and Count Vol ney, and many of them proficients in its ribaldry and bawdy habits. The "Father of his country" was a prominent object of their intrigues and reproaches. The soul of Washington was never so near despair for his country as when he was then at times overburdened with the responsibilities and fears arising from such a state of things. Intemperance was universal, and indulged in to so terrible a degree of license as would now seem incredible. Whisky was almost the sole production of extensive new regions. "A horse could only carry four bushels of rye, but he could carry the whisky made from twenty-four bushels." To defend it from taxation was the cause of the Rebellion of 1794 against the Federal authority. "Whisky," said a distinguished French officer, "is the best part of the American government." Many of the pulpits of the country were filled by a formal and worldly ministry, or by men who had fled from the ecclesiastical censures of the lands across the sea. The Church was, where it existed, generally conformed to the gay society about it. The picture of portions of the region bordering on the Ohio, by Rev. Dr. Joseph Doddridge, was applicable to the principal part of the West and South. He states: "Among the people with whom I was most conversant there was no other vestige of the Christian religion than a faint observation of Sunday, and that merely as a day of rest for the aged and a play-day for the young."

Nor did God leave himself without witness of his displeasure. Some remarkable chastisements were inflicted upon the nation. One of them was the yellow fever, which ravaged extensively the Northern as well as the Southern coasts. Philadelphia was visited five times by it between 1793 and 1802. Other epidemics spread elsewhere, among the most terrible the small-pox. This strange, hideous and fatal disease seems in its history almost like a messenger of wrath sent from God to chastise the world and prepare the way for great reformations. The Sandwich Islanders thus class it with, and name it, "leprosy." It can be traced back in Eastern Asia to the age corresponding to that of the judges in Israel. It marched with Mohammedanism over Asia and Europe—with the Spaniards into the New World.* It has been in later times the chief of "the four great eruptive diseases" which are supposed to cause "one-ninth of the total mortality" of mankind. (*Rayer: Diseases of the Skin.*) At the close of the last century so prevalent did it become that the deaths from it as compared with those from all other diseases increased twenty-five per cent. *Sir Gilbert Blaine* says that "in the year 1800 the small-pox had broken out twenty times in the Channel fleet alone." But God mercifully interposed: first, inoculation, which was brought to England in 1772, and then the sovereign specific, vaccination, discovered by Dr. Edward Jenner in 1796, set bounds to its fury.

The General Assembly in its pastoral letter of 1798 uses the language of great dejection, alarm and expostulation in addressing "the people in their communion." They say "formidable innovations and convulsions in Europe threaten destruction to morals and religion; scenes of devastation and bloodshed, unexampled in the history of modern nations, have convulsed the world, and our country is threatened with similar calamities." "We perceive, with pain and fearful apprehension, a general dereliction of religious principle and practice among our fellow-citizens, a visible and prevailing impiety and contempt for

* It was estimated that three and a half millions of the people of Mexico were swept off by this awful scourge.

the laws and institutions of religion, and an abounding infidelity which in many instances tends to Atheism itself." "The profligacy and corruption of the public morals have advanced with a progress proportioned to our declension in religion. Profaneness, pride, luxury, injustice, intemperance, lewdness and every species of debauchery and loose indulgence greatly abound." They address to the churches some most solemn exhortations, and appoint the last Thursday of August as a day of humiliation, fasting and prayer, upon which this letter is to be read from every pulpit, accompanied with suitable discourses from the ministers.

CHAPTER III.

BEGINNINGS OF REVIVAL.

IT was by the permission of such general gloom, apostasy and profligacy that the Holy Spirit was showing to the sincere followers of God the evil and deadly nature of sin, their own utter helplessness and their dependence upon God alone for salvation, and was compelling them to cry before him with abasement and importunity for the gifts of his grace. And were prayers ever lifted before him in such abasement, sense of need, confidence in his mercy and reliance on the all-sufficient atonement and intercession of Jesus Christ, to which abundant answers were not given? It is "when the enemy comes in like a flood," and threatens to overrun and sweep away all that is precious, that "the Spirit of the Lord lifts up a standard," causes the trumpet to be sounded, rallies his followers, and bestows the most sudden, overwhelming and glorious triumphs. So Israel of old ever found; so we find it now.

It is to be remarked distinctly, for the comfort and encouragement of the portions of the Church whose circumstances are most trying, that the scenes which, during these darkest years of our country's history, were visited by marks of God's favor were chiefly amidst the new settlements, where the greatest hardships and dangers were experienced, and the scattered and tried families of his followers most needed, and most earnestly sought, his help. The Great Revival of 1800 affected the whole country, but was most powerfully felt in the region extending from the Allegheny Mountains westward to the borders of civilization, and in the Southern States.

There were occasional revivals during the latter years of the Revolution, and subsequently in several parts of the country, but preparatory showers of the great rain may be most distinctly traced in a succession of visitations of divine grace upon the churches of the new settlements of Western Pennsylvania. The people of that region were chiefly Presbyterians from the north of Ireland and from Scotland. "They were (says *Dr. E. H. Gillett*, in his *History of the Presbyterian Church*) by no means the miscellaneous driftwood which emigration usually floats off from older communities to new settlements. Among them were men of culture, and a large proportion of them were characterized by stern religious principle. They were men whose energy and vigor were developed by the circumstances of their lot, and who, in grappling with the forest and repelling or guarding against savage attacks, were made more sagacious, fearless and self-reliant." Their "hearts beat as true to the cause of freedom, intelligence, morals and religion as any in the world."

The following account of these first beginnings of the wonderful work of grace is given by the late *Rev. Joseph Stevenson*, of Ohio:

"It may almost be said that the Presbyterian Church in Western Pennsylvania was born in a revival. In 1778

Vance's Fort, into which the families living adjacent had been driven by the Indians, was the scene of a remarkable work. There was but one pious man in the fort, Joseph Patterson, a layman, an earnest and devoted Christian, whose zeal had not waned even amid the storm and terrors of war; and during the long days and nights of their besiegement he talked with his careless associates of an enemy more to be dreaded than the Indian, and a death more terrible than by the scalping-knife. As they were shut up within very narrow limits, his voice, though directed to one or two, could easily be heard by the whole company, and thus his personal exhortations became public addresses. Deep seriousness filled every breast, and some twenty persons were there led to Christ. These were a short time subsequently formed into the Cross Creek church, which built its house of worship near the fort, and had as its pastor for thirty-three years one of these converts, the Rev. Thomas Marquis.

"From 1781 to 1787 a more extensive work of grace was experienced in the churches of Cross Creek, Upper Buffalo, Chartiers, Pigeon Creek, Bethel, Lebanon, Ten Mile, Cross Roads and Mill Creek, during which *more than a thousand* persons were brought into the kingdom of Christ. Considering the unsettled state of the public mind at the close of the Revolutionary war, the constant anxiety and watchfulness against the incursions of hostile Indians, the toils and hardships incident to new settlements, and the scarcity of ministers, this was a signal work of the Spirit, greatly strengthening the feeble churches."

A fuller narrative of these more limited effusions of the

Holy Spirit was prepared by a committee of the Presbytery, and published in the *Western Missionary Magazine*, which was begun in the town of Washington, Pa., in 1803.

"In the latter part of the year 1781, the Lord began a gracious work in the congregations of Cross Creek and Upper Buffalo, under the ministry of the Rev. Joseph Smith, about one year after he took the pastoral care of these congregations. During the winter season, week-day and night sermons and meetings for social worship were frequent, the assemblies numerous and attentive, and a considerable number under deep convictions, with frequent instances of new awakenings. The summer following was remarkable for the increase of the number of the awakened, although most labored long without relief. The few pious persons who were in these infant congregations were at this time earnestly engaged for additions to their number, and felt something of the pangs of travailing in birth for souls; much of the spirit of prayer was poured out. In the latter part of this summer the work became more glorious and comfortable; numbers of the distressed souls obtained sweet deliverance; and at the time the Lord's Supper was administered in Buffalo, in the fall of 1783, about one hundred of the subjects of this good work were admitted to communion, and many were awakened on that solemn occasion. The awakening and hopeful conversion of sinners continued and increased through three or four years; nor was there much appearance of a decline for six or seven years after it began.

"Within this gracious season there were many sweet, solemn sacramental occasions. The most remarkable of these was at Cross Creek, in the spring of the year 1787. It was a very refreshing season to the pious, a time of deliverance to a number of the distressed and of awakening to many. The Monday evening was peculiarly and awfully solemn; some hundreds were bowed down and silently weeping, and a few crying out in anguish of soul. After the solemn dismission of the assembly most of the people remained on the ground; the scene was very remarkable; the pious were generally joyful and lively, sinners greatly alarmed, and many deeply distressed. The people, unwilling to part, did not leave the place till an hour or more in the night, when they parted with an appointment to meet there again the next morning. Tuesday was indeed a solemn day; it was spent chiefly in exhortations and prayers by the Rev. Messrs. Smith, Dod and Cornwell. The effects of this gracious visitation were very comfortable, producing a good harvest of souls. Upward of fifty in these congregations were added to the church at the communion the next fall.

"Nearly about the same time in which this gracious work began in these congregations, the divine influences were also poured out upon the congregations of Chartiers and Pigeon Creek, under the ministry of the Rev. John McMillan; many were awakened, and the pious much revived and quickened. There were a goodly number of judicious Christians in these congregations who actively stepped forward in their proper places, and were very helpful in carrying on the good work. As many attended from considerable distances, with a great thirst for ordinances, it was thought expedient to have social meetings for prayer and exhortation on the Sabbath nights; they generally continued all the night; many attended, and conviction and conversion work went graciously on. Frequently the exercised could not suppress their feelings of joy or distress, but gave them vent in groans and cries. There were also frequently week-day and night sermons and societies in different parts of the congregations. Thus this good work went on for several years, and it is believed that many were brought savingly to close with Christ in these congregations; and it is evident, from a trial of near twenty years, that the work is real and genuine with respect to some hundreds in those two charges above stated, many of whom are now faithful leaders, zealous and active Christians and pillars in the church of Christ.

"In the same time whilst this gracious work was going on in those places, the Lord also poured out his Spirit on several other neighboring congregations, particularly Bethel and Lebanon, under the ministry of the Rev. John Clarke; Ten Mile, under the ministry of the Rev. Thaddeus Dod; and King's Creek and Mill Creek, then vacant congregations. In all of these places the power of God was graciously displayed, and many souls gathered in who have since given evidence in their lives and conversation that the work with them was a reality and of divine original.

"We are able to state, from particular acquaintance and frequent conversation with some hundreds of those who were exercised during this happy season of gracious visitation in all the above places, that in general their distress arose from a deep sense of the contrariety of their hearts and lives to the law of God, and the awful wages of sin, which they saw they were in imminent danger of receiving, of their utter indisposition to turn to God, to love his law, or embrace Jesus Christ, by reason of the hardness of their hearts, blindness of their minds and enmity against God. The peace and consolations of those who obtained relief did not arise from a view of either their hearts or lives being less offensive to God, or from their having done any thing recommending or entitling them to the divine notice or favor, nor merely from a persuasion of God's having pardoned their sins, but from a scriptural discovery of the plan of salvation by free, sovereign grace, through the obedience, sufferings and death of Jesus Christ, the God-man, which they viewed suitable to their perishing condition, and to every valuable purpose; and they found their wills gained over to the cordial choice of this plan, and that their souls became delighted with the character and holy law of God.

"In the year 1795 there was a gracious shower of the divine influence in the congregation of Chartiers, which occasioned a considerable reviving and ingathering of souls. In this visitation the Academy at Canonsburg shared largely. About forty-five were added to the Church.

"In the year 1799 refreshing showers of divine influence were poured on many congregations in the bounds of our Presbytery, in which several hundreds were added to the Church.

"Those congregations which had pastors very generally shared in this gracious visit, and also some that were vacant were refreshed and strengthened.

"In each of the above mentioned seasons of gracious visitation, and in the several places mentioned, numbers discountenanced and opposed the good work; but very few publicly, or with such weight as to occasion any considerable disturbance or difficulty.

"This work throughout was generally carried on in the more ordinary or mild and moderate manner. Although convictions were deep and pungent, the sense of sin, guilt and danger very affecting, and the apprehensions of divine wrath distressing, yet they were not attended with any extraordinary bodily affections, but in few, if any, instances. The work was also remarkably free from enthusiasm, wild imaginations, and disorderly, hurtful irregularities. Although there have been some instances of apostasy, yet it must be remarked, to the praise of free grace, that these have been but few amongst those respecting whom their pious friends and the officers of the Church entertained a favorable opinion that they had been the subjects of saving grace, and who were admitted to the communion of the Church.

"In the interims of the gracious visitations which have been noticed there were some sad degrees of declension; perhaps more especially and generally after the last mentioned season, in 1799, when the graceless became more bold in sin and impiety, the floods of vanity and carnality appeared likely to carry all before them; most of the pious became very weak and feeble in the cause of Christ, much buried in and carried away with the things and pursuits of the world, and in some places a spirit of contention and animosity crept in, which appeared to lead into a great degree of contempt of ordinances and government in the church and in families. Here, however, we are again called to remark, to the praise of free grace, that God still so kept his hand about his Church, his cause and his people that those means and ordinances which God had peculiarly countenanced and made effectual in his work were still generally maintained. The ministers in general were enabled faithfully to declare the counsel of God, and in plainness, with honesty and simplicity, to hold forth the doctrines of grace, and there was generally considerable solemnity in the time of dispensing the word and ordinances, but the effects appeared not to be abiding, save with a few. Meetings for social worship, which the Lord very specially owned and blessed in the times of reviving, were, in the darkest times, in most places kept up, though not so frequent nor so generally attended. The meeting for concert prayer for the outpouring of the Spirit of revival of religion, on the first Tuesday in every quarter of the year, was cordially entered into by the Ohio Presbytery, and practiced generally throughout their bounds since the beginning of the year 1796. Thus there was, for the most part, some attention to the means kept up, though, alas! too generally they appeared as barren ordinances."

CHAPTER IV.

WONDERFUL COMMUNION SCENES.

THE committee of Presbytery, in the *Magazine* previously mentioned, describes some scenes at communions of the churches in Washington County, Pennsylvania, which seemed like a renewal of the Day of Pentecost, and have rarely had a parallel in any subsequent age.

"About the latter end of the year 1801, and beginning of 1802, there was a remarkable attendance upon ordinances; meetings for the worship of God, both public and social, were generally crowded, and there appeared an increasing attention to the word and great solemnity in the assemblies. The people of God became more sensible of and affected with the low state of religion, and the dangerous, perishing condition of sinners. It appeared that God made use of the intelligence we had of the revival of religion in other places to excite a longing and praying for the Lord's returning with power to our languishing churches, that we might experience the displays of his power and grace which he was making in other parts. Desire and prayer for this great favor increased through the following winter in many of our congregations, and in the spring and first part of the summer of 1802 there was a considerable rising of expectation that the Lord would not altogether forsake or pass us by, but that he would yet favor us with a gracious visitation; and indeed we were blest with some tokens of his presence in his ordinances. Not only the children of God were more quickened and aroused, but also in many instances there appeared to be an alarm and some concern amongst unregenerate sinners. These appearances were considerably increased at the time of the sacramental seasons, more especially perhaps at Cross Creek and Lower Buffalo toward the last of June. On both of these occasions the children of God were much quickened and revived, numbers of sinners brought under serious concern, and some hopefully led to rest on Christ. On the Monday in particular at Lower Buffalo there was evidence of the presence and power of God. It was difficult to part after two discourses were delivered. The preaching appeared to come home to the heart with power, and singing a parting hymn at the conclusion greatly affected many. The pious appeared to go away from this place with lively expectations that the time to favor this part of our Zion was drawing near. From this time it appeared that almost every meeting, sermon or society, through the divine blessing, produced new effects, particularly leading to the work of examination and inquiry into the grounds of controversy which prevented the gracious visitation of the Lord, and exciting to more earnest wrestling and pleading with God for the effusion of his Spirit and display of his power and grace; and it was evident that for this purpose a spirit of prayer and supplication was given to many. Thus it appears that the Lord was, through the summer, preparing his way for his coming to this part of his church, to make those displays of his power and grace which we have since witnessed and experienced.

"In the month of September, 1802, the Lord began in a glorious manner to show his stately steppings in the sanctuaries of his grace. At several sacramental occasions in that month there were considerable evidences of the gracious presence of God, and of the operations of his Holy Spirit. But the first extraordinary manifestations of the Divine power were made in the congregation of the Three Springs, part of the charge of the Rev. Elisha Macurdy, at the time of the administration of the Lord's Supper, on the fourth Sabbath of September, 1802. For some weeks before, there had been in this congregation more appearance of solemnity and serious exercise than usual. There had been also, among the pious in both congregations, for some time, an uncommon engagedness in pleading for the divine presence on that occasion. It is thought not improper to mention, for the encouragement of others in future, that an agreement was made and attended to by them to spend a certain time, about sun-setting, on each Thursday, in secret prayer, each by themselves, to plead with God for his gracious presence and the outpouring of his Spirit on that occasion. This was done for some weeks before the Sacrament. On the Sabbath immediately preceding the communion there was considerable evidence of the powerful presence of God, particularly toward the close of the afternoon sermon. When the congregation was dismissed, about fifty persons continued upon the ground, appeared unwilling to go away, and spent the most of the night in social worship.

"On Thursday following, which was observed as a fast in preparation for the Lord's Supper, the impressions still increased. Society was appointed in the evening; a considerable number attended, and before worship began two young persons, who had retired to the woods to pray, fell to the ground, unable to bear up any longer under the distressing anguish of a wounded spirit. Their cries for mercy were very affecting. After some time two persons went to them and inquired the cause of their distress. Their reply was, that they were exposed to the wrath of God. When Christ was proposed to them as a remedy, their reply was, that their hearts were at enmity against God, and they could not accept of him, although they were sure they would be damned without an interest in him; besides, they had so long rejected salvation, they were now afraid God would not have mercy on them. Most of the time from that until Saturday at one o'clock was spent in conversing with the distressed. Their general complaint was a sense of guilt, especially in rejecting Christ; hardness of heart and inability to help themselves; and all acknowledged the justice of God in their condemnation. As yet there were no instances of deliverance.

"Saturday was a time of gracious influences; many more were brought under concern. Most of that night was spent in social worship, and the work remarkably increased until Monday morning. When the congregation was dismissed, some hundreds remained; several attempts were made to part, but all in vain. They remained all night on the ground; and this night far exceeded any that had been before. About the break of day on Tuesday morning there were six persons who gave evidence of obtaining hope in Jesus. About eleven o'clock the assembly dispersed. On the Thursday following the people of the Cross Road congregation, the other part of Mr. Macurdy's charge, met for social worship, it being their monthly society day. This was also a time of God's power. There were many instances of new awakening. They continued all the night in religious exercises."

"On Tuesday, the 5th of October, 1802, the day of concerted prayer, the Lord appeared, by the powerful operation of the Spirit, in the congregation of Cross Creek, the charge of the Rev. Thomas Marquis. The people were solemn and attentive through the day, and in the evening, when dismissed, they appeared backward to go away. After part were gone and many standing about the doors, one of the elders who was in the house went to the door and spoke a few words respecting their situation, and in a few minutes the young people were all in tears. They then joined in singing a hymn and in prayer. By this time some of those who had gone away returned. They went all again into the house, candles were brought, and the night was spent in prayer, conversation and praise, until two o'clock in the morning. During this time many cried out in the anguish of their souls, bitterly lamenting their misimprovement of time and abuse of mercies. They, in a very moving manner, expressed their sense of sin and guilt, the hardness of their hearts and the justice of God in passing them by neglected in this their deep distress; they freely acknowledged their bitter malice and violent opposition which they had felt and indulged in their hearts against God's work and people. Some confessed that they had come in the most contemptuous manner to the house of God that day, with a professed intention to get the people of God to pray for them; but were then astonished that God had not made them monuments of his divine vengeance, upon account of their rejecting the Lord Jesus Christ, and other heaven-daring wickedness.

"The next day there was a meeting on the outline of the congregation, adjoining Mr. Macurdy's congregation. The people were silent in the time of divine service, with a few exceptions; but when the congregation was dismissed the effects of God's power more visibly appeared. Many then cried out in great agony of soul; many more expressed their concern by a desire of social worship that night, in which they were gratified. The house, though of a middle size, was not sufficient to contain the people, on which account many went away after a short sermon. The exercises of prayer and praise, with frequent exhortations, continued the whole night, except two short intervals spent in conversation with the distressed. This was a very solemn season; the people were almost universally bowed, while some appeared to be upon the brink of despair. Some few obtained relief before day, who have since given evidence of serious and comfortable exercise. A goodly number who since that time have been admitted to the table of the Lord have dated their first deep and abiding convictions from that season. It was a night to be had in everlasting remembrance, for which it is hoped many will praise God eternally. At this time some began to speak the language of Canaan with solemn sweet serenity of mind, and in heavenly heart-affecting accents.

"On the Sabbath following, which was the 10th day of October, 1802, the Lord's Supper was administered at Racoon congregation, the charge of the Rev. Joseph Patterson. As many as the house could contain attended to social worship and preaching throughout the night. Divine worship was also carried on a considerable part of the night at the tent; many new awakenings took place through the night, and the social exercises continued until the public worship began on Monday. Through this day many more were made to cry out in agony of soul, unable to sit or stand; some of them, very notorious in vanity and profanity, were struck to the ground and constrained to cry out aloud in bitter anguish of soul, 'Undone! undone! for ever undone!' Some who were considerably advanced in years were in this situation, as well as many younger, who were crying for mercy, some of whom had been ring-leaders in wickedness and impiety, conducting with the greatest insolence and contempt. Toward evening the exercise was particularly solemn and powerful; several persons of Racoon congregation were at this time awakened; few or none of this congregation had appeared to be awakened before.

"The last Sabbath in October the Lord's Supper was administered at Cross Roads. A great multitude of people collected; many from a great distance, accommodated with provisions to continue on the ground during the whole of the solemnity. There were thirty-two wagons. On Sabbath day and night there was much rain and snow; yet the people mostly continued at the place night and day until

Tuesday morning. Nine ministers attended. The meeting-house, though large, being insufficient to contain half the people, the Sacrament was administered at the tent to about eight hundred communicants—of whom forty-one were then admitted for the first time—of the Cross Roads and Three Springs congregations. Though there was a continual fall of rain this large assembly attended with undisturbed composure. In order to accommodate the multitude two action sermons were preached. The communicants then removed to the communion table at the tent. A great many were affected, and some had to be assisted to move out.

"Ministers still preached successively in the house throughout the day. Prayers and exhortations were continued all night in the meeting-house, except at short intervals, when a speaker's voice could not be heard for the cries and groans of the distressed.

"On Monday three ministers preached at different places, one in the house and two out in the encampments. This was a very solemn day, particularly in the house. After public worship was concluded and the people were preparing to remove, the scene was very affecting. The house was thronged full, and when some of those without were about to go away, they found that part of their families were in the house, and some of them lying in distress, unable to remove. This prevented a general removal; and though a number went away, the greater part remained. About the time of the departure of those who went away, the work became more powerful than it had been at any time before, and numbers who had prepared to go were constrained to stay. It was a memorable time of the displays of Divine power and grace through the whole night. Many of the young people were remarkably exercised, and frequently addressed others about the perishing condition they were in—the glories of the Saviour—the excellency and suitableness of the plan of salvation—and warned, invited and pressed sinners to come to Christ; all this in a manner quite astonishing for their years. Numbers of old experienced Christians also were particularly exercised, were much refreshed and comforted, and affectingly recommended the Lord Jesus and his religion to those around them. About sunrise, after a time of solemn, sweet exercise, the congregation was dismissed, and soon after dispersed.

"Shortly before this sacramental season, numbers of the exercised in Cross Creek and other congregations obtained some relief to their troubled minds. Opportunities were taken to converse with them, and a number were found to have gotten ease and obtained hopes which did not appear to be well founded. This excited some alarm among the pious and discerning, and gave occasion to make the most careful discrimination between conviction and conversion—a true and a false peace—when treating the subject of soul exercise, both in public administration and private conversation, and to guard against error, delusion and enthusiasm. And here we must acknowledge, to the glory of sovereign grace, that God owned and blessed feeble attempts of this kind to rectify the mistakes of poor young sinners caught in Satan's net. In some instances three or four persons have on Sabbath evenings and other occasions acknowledged their deceptions, and blessed God for discovering to them their error; and their convictions returned and became more rational, deep and abiding, and their exercises more scriptural.

"The gracious manifestations which the Lord made of his presence on this precious season at the Cross Roads, and his countenancing the appointment by awakening many who came from distant congregations, induced the making of an appointment for the administration of the Lord's Supper again, at Upper Buffalo, on the second Sabbath of November.

"In the interim the work considerably increased where it had been, and began in other places on the return of those who had been to the Cross Roads, of whom many had been made the subjects of the work while there. The sweet savor and the power of the Holy Spirit continued with them when they returned home, and they were made the happy instruments of awakening and engaging others in the congregations where they dwelt.

"On Saturday, the 13th day of November, 1802, a greater concourse of people than had ever been seen before at a meeting for divine worship in this country assembled at Upper Buffalo meeting-house, in the congregation of the Rev. John Anderson, and formed an encampment in a semi-circle around the front of the tent, in a shady wood. The greater part had by this time learned from experience the necessity of coming prepared to encamp on the ground during the solemnity, as so many persons in distress could not be removed to lodgings in the evening; nor could such a multitude be accommodated in a neighborhood of the most hospitable inhabitants, taking all home to lodgings. On this occasion it would have required one hundred houses, with perhaps one hundred persons to each house. But the people had been so engaged that they were not disposed to separate in the evenings; therefore many brought wagons (about fifty of them) with their families and provisions, with a great number of tents, which they pitched for their accommodation. The public exercises of devotion commenced at two o'clock, with sermons both in the meeting-house and at the tent, and were continued, with but short intermissions, until Tuesday evening. Fifteen ministers were present, all members of the Synod of Pittsburg, and with cordial harmony took part in the various labors of the solemn season. The administration of the word and ordinances was accompanied with an extraordinary effusion of Divine influence on the hearts of the hearers. Some hundreds were, during the season, convicted of their sin and misery. Preaching, exhortations, prayers and praises, were continued alternately throughout the whole night in the meeting-house, which was crowded full, and also part of the night at the tent.

"On the Sabbath morning, action sermons were preached in the meeting-house and at the tent; and after the way was prepared at both places, the communicants from the house repaired to the communion table at the tent, where the holy ordinance was administered to about nine hundred and sixty communicants. The solemn scene was conducted with as much regularity as usual, and with much solemnity and affection. The multitude of non-communicants who could not hear at the tent were called to the meeting-house and to a shady grove, where they were addressed by several ministers during the administration of the ordinance.

"This night was spent as the former had been; perhaps the only difference that appeared was in the numbers who were visibly pierced to the heart, and made to cry out, *What shall we do?* and in the degree of their exercise, both of which greatly exceeded those of the preceding night.

"Between midnight and day-break, after a short intermission of public worship, an exhortation was given to the distressed, directing them to Christ, and setting forth the fullness of his grace and suitableness to all their wants.

"On Monday the whole assembly was addressed by one speaker from the tent. They were composed, solemn and attentive during the time of public worship; but after the blessing was pronounced, many were struck down in all parts of the congregation, and many more sat still, silently weeping over their miserable state as sinners exposed to eternal wrath. Many of God's dear children were filled with peace in believing. They saw the spiritual glory which the gracious presence of God had given to the solemnity; they rejoiced in hope, and waited to see and feel more of the efficacy of free grace. Others, sorrowful and thirsting for the water of life, wished to stay a little longer at the pool. The ministers, therefore, determined not to leave them, but to labor with diligence while God was making the word and ordinances effectual to the conviction and conversion of sinners. Not a few were awakened to a lively sense of their sin during the evening and night, who have since, we hope, obtained pardon and peace with God through our Lord Jesus Christ. The exercises were continued until after sunrise on Tuesday morning, when the assembly was solemnly dismissed, and began with apparent reluctance to prepare to disperse. Notwithstanding that they had continued so long and rested little, it appeared to be very difficult to separate and leave the place. After some time the most removed, except the people of the congregation, who still tarried, lingering at the place where so much of God's power had been manifested to their eyes and in their consciences. Numbers, who had gone home to provide refreshments for their friends, returned. Still they could not part. All again collected in the meeting-house, where this day also was spent till evening in preaching, exhortation and prayer. The exercise was very powerful, and numbers were affected who appeared to be unmoved before."

One of the most powerful sermons on this Pentecostal occasion was an exposition of the second Psalm, by Rev. Elisha Macurdy, which was long known in the region round as "Macurdy's war sermon." "The scene," said Rev. Thomas Hunt, who was in the wagon from which it was preached, "appeared to me like the close of a battle in which every tenth man had been fatally wounded. The recollection thrills through my soul while I write." (*Rev. Dr. D. Elliott: Life of Macurdy.*)

The churches from Lake Erie southward along the western side of the Allegheny Mountains, and through the few settled portions of the North-west Territory, which about this time were formed into the State of Ohio, felt the swelling of the river of the water of life. The first Presbyterian Church formed in Eastern Ohio was blessed, according to this narrative of the Presbytery of Ohio, with a share of the refreshing influences. It says: "In the latter end of the year 1798 the Lord poured out his Spirit on a new settlement, on the north-west of the Ohio river, between the Great and the Little Beavers, since formed into two congregations under the pastoral care of the Rev. Thomas E. Hughes, under whose first ministrations amongst them this good work began. The operations of the Holy Spirit in this place were very powerful, and in many instances hopefully successful. In a short space of time a considerable number, we trust, were made the subjects of a saving work of grace. In this work an English school in that place shared very graciously. The youth or children who attended it were generally exercised for a considerable time, so much so that all play and diversions were stopped, and the intervals were spent in reading, conversing about their souls' concerns, singing hymns or retiring into the woods to pray. It is believed that eighteen out of thirty in this school were made the subjects of divine grace. In the August following, the Sacrament of the Supper was administered in that place, which was the first time on that side of the Ohio river,* when about thirty of the subjects of this work were admitted to communion."

* This refers only to South-eastern Ohio. The Rev. Daniel Story was preaching and no doubt administering the Sacraments of the Church at Marietta and vicinity, in 1791; Rev. James Kemper, at Cincinnati, in the same year; and Rev. William Speer, who had resigned prospects of much usefulness in Chambersburg and elsewhere, and accepted of an invitation to erect the standard of the Cross at Chillicothe, which was then the seat of government of the whole of the North-west Territory, planted the first church there in 1798.

CHAPTER V.

ASTONISHING OUTPOURINGS IN THE SOUTH.

THE early settlers of Kentucky were a wild race, many of them but little instructed in the word of God, and paying little respect to the ordinances of the gospel. The godly David Rice, who went there in 1783, says of them (*Memoirs*), "I found scarcely one man, and but few women, who supported a credible profession of religion. Some were grossly ignorant of the first principles of religion; some were given to quarreling and fighting, some to intemperance, and perhaps most of them totally ignorant of the forms of religion in their own houses." And yet "many of them produced certificates of having been in full communion and in good standing in the churches from which they had emigrated." Here was a material capable of being kindled into the most violent excitement by a certain measure of the genuine influences of the Holy Spirit, alarming their fears, or showing them their backslidden state, and peculiarly liable, through ignorance, to plunge into fanatical errors.

Some of the scenes witnessed in Kentucky are almost beyond our conception. An eyewitness of a vast meeting at Cane Ridge, in August, 1801, to which people had come from all quarters of the State, even the distance of two hundred miles, and from the settlements north of the Ohio, thus describes it: "We arrived upon the ground, and here a scene presented itself to my mind, not only novel and unaccountable, but awful beyond description. A vast crowd, supposed by some to have amounted to twenty-five thousand, was collected together. The noise was like the roar of Niagara. The vast sea of human beings seemed to be agitated by a storm. I counted seven preachers, all preaching at one time, some on stumps, others on wagons." (*Rev. J. B. Finley, Autobiography.*) The shouting, shrieking, praying and nervous spasms of this vast multitude produced an unearthly and almost terrible spectacle. The religious exercises on the ground were continued from Friday morning until the ensuing Wednesday evening, day and night, without intermission. Heavy rains fell during that time, apparently without being noticed by the people, though few were protected by any covering.

From such a tempest of religious emotions much evil resulted. Campbellism and Universalism have been cast forth like a scum. The Presbyterian Church itself was rent asunder, and the "Cumberland" branch of it, holding semi-Arminian doctrine, and licensing uneducated men to preach, arose there. And these masses of people were convulsed by inexplicable nervous affections of a spasmodic nature. Still, from the inflammable chaff much wheat was sifted, which has borne precious seed and been gathered with rejoicing.

A fair conception of the meetings in the more sober parts of the South-west may be obtained from the following letter, written by *Rev. James McGready*, descriptive of some held in *Tennessee:*

"The present summer (viz., 1800) has been the most glorious time that our guilty eyes have ever beheld. All the blessed displays of Almighty power and grace, all the sweet gales of the divine Spirit and soul-reviving showers of the blessings of heaven, which we enjoyed before, and which we considered wonderful beyond conception, were but like a few scattering drops before the mighty rain which Jehovah has poured out like a mighty river upon this our guilty, unworthy country. The Lord has indeed showed himself a prayer-hearing God; he has given his people a praying spirit and a lively faith, and then he has answered their prayers far beyond their highest expectations. This wilderness and solitary place has been made glad, this dreary desert now rejoices and blossoms like the rose; yea, it blossoms abundantly, and rejoices even with joy and singing.

"At Gasper river, on the fourth Sabbath of June, a surprising multitude of people collected, many from a very great distance, even from the distance of thirty to sixty, and one hundred miles. On Friday and Saturday there was a very solemn attention. On Saturday evening, after the congregation was dismissed, as a few serious, exercised Christians were sitting conversing together, and appeared to be more than commonly engaged, the flame started from them and overspread the whole house until every person appeared less or more engaged. The greater part of the ministers and several hundreds of the people remained at the meeting-house all night. Through every part of the multitude there could be found some awakened souls struggling in the pangs of the new birth, ready to faint and die for Christ, almost upon the brink of desperation. Others again were just lifted from the horrible pit, and beginning to lisp the first notes of the new song, and to tell the sweet wonders which they saw in Christ. Ministers and experienced Christians were everywhere engaged praying, exhorting, conversing and trying to lead inquiring souls to the Lord Jesus. In this exercise the night was spent till near the break of day. The Sabbath was a blessed day in every sense of the word. The groans of awakened sinners could be heard all over the house during the morning sermon, but by no means so as to disturb the assembly. It was a comfortable time with many at the table. Mr. McGee preached in the evening upon the account of Peter's sinking in the waves. In the application of his sermon the power of God seemed to shake the whole assembly. Toward the close of the sermon the cries of the distressed arose almost as loud as his voice. After the congregation was dismissed the solemnity increased till the greater part of the multitude seemed engaged in the most solemn manner. No person appeared to wish to go home; hunger and sleep seemed to affect nobody. Eternal things were the vast concern. Here awakening and converting work was to be found in every part of the multitude, and even some things strangely and wonderfully new to me. Sober professors, who had been communicants for many years, now lying prostrate on the ground, crying out in such language as this: 'I have been a sober professor, I have been a communicant; O, I have been deceived, I have no religion.' The greater part of the multitude continued at the meeting-house all night, and no person appeared uneasy for food or sleep.

"On Monday a vast concourse of people came together. This was another day of the Son of Man. With propriety we could adopt the language of the patriarch, and say, 'The Lord is here: how dreadful is this place! It is none other but the house of God and the very gate of heaven!' Two powerful sermons were preached by Messrs. McGee and Hodge. The almighty power of God attended the word to the hearts of many, and a universal solemnity overspread the whole assembly. When the congregation was dismissed, no person seemed to wish to leave the place. The solemnity increased, and conviction seemed to spread from heart to heart. Little children, young men and women, and old gray-headed people, persons of every description, white and black, were to be found in every part of the multitude, pricked to the heart with clear, rational, scriptural convictions, crying out for mercy in the most extreme distress; whilst every now and then we could find one and another delivered from their burden of sin and guilt by sweet believing views of the glory of God in the face of Jesus Christ. In such exercises the multitude continued at the meeting-house till Tuesday morning after sunrise, when they broke up after they were dismissed by prayer, and indeed the circumstance of their parting added to the solemnity of the occasion. The number that, we hope, were savingly brought to Christ on this occasion were forty-five persons."

The population of *North Carolina* was largely Presbyterian. The persecutions at the beginning of the last century drove many of the Scotch to take refuge in the two Carolinas. There they cherished a love of freedom, made the more ardent by the memory of their own sufferings. There was a warm religious sympathy between them and the Presbyterians of Pennsylvania. Ministers often passed from the one section to the other.

In 1788, James McGready, a pupil of Dr. McMillan, of Canonsburgh, was licensed to preach by the Presbytery of Redstone. He possessed much of his teacher's strong and energetic character and fervent zeal, kindled by the fire of the earlier revivals. He soon afterward went to North Carolina, where he had spent some of his earlier years, and commenced preaching with a power which earned him the name of "Boanerges." He went from there to Tennessee and Kentucky in 1796. His terrible denunciations of prevalent sins and plain expositions of the only way of salvation prepared the way for a deep interest in the later revival in the regions north and west, and for the rapid communication of its influences.

One of the most memorable scenes in its course in North Carolina was witnessed at a communion in Orange County. Rev. Dr. W. H. Foote, in his *Sketches of North Carolina*, thus describes it:

"In August, 1801, a communion season was held at Cross Roads in Orange County. The stated minister, Wm. Paisley, was assisted by Rev. Dr. Caldwell and Rev. Leonard Prather, and two young licentiates, Hugh Shaw and Ebenezer B. Currie. Nothing of especial interest appeared in the congregation during the days preceding the Sabbath, or during the administration of the ordinance. Great solemnity prevailed, mingled with evident anxiety as well as prayer, among Christians, that God would bless the congregation and revive his work. On Monday, the 28th, the public services were conducted by Messrs. Prather and Shaw, without any expression or appearance of emotion among the people. The pastor arose to dismiss the people, intending first to say a few words expressive of his sorrow that apparently no advance had been made in bringing sinners to God. Overwhelmed with his sensations of distress that God had imparted no blessings to his people, he stood silent a few moments and then sat down. A solemn stillness pervaded the congregation. In a few moments he rose again; before he uttered a word, a young man from Tennessee, who had been interested in the revival there, and had been telling the people of Cross Roads during the meeting much about the state of things in the West, raised up his hands and cried out, 'Stand still and see the salvation of God!' In a few moments the silence was broken by sobs, groans and cries, rising commingled from all parts of the house. All thoughts of dismissing the congregation at once vanished. The remainder of the day was spent in the exercises of prayer, exhortation, singing and personal conversation, and midnight came before the congregation could be persuaded to go to their respective homes. The excitement continued for a length of time, and many were hopefully converted to God. No irregularities appeared in this commencement of the great excitement in North Carolina; the sobs and groans and cries for mercy were unusual, but seemed justified by the deep feeling of individuals on account of the great interests concerned.

"In October following, the usual fall communion was held in Hawfields, the other part of Mr. Paisley's charge. The expression of feeling was great from the first; the people from Cross Roads were there in their fervency of excitement and hope, and multitudes, whom the report of what had been done at the August meeting drew together, were full of expectation, some wondering and some seeking their salvation. People from a distance came in their wagons and remained on the ground all night. The meeting was continued for five days without intermission, the various religious services of prayer, singing, sermons, exhortations and personal conversations succeeding each other, with short intervals of refreshment, during the day, and a few hours for sleep during the night. Impressions of a religious nature were very general and very deep, and in a great multitude of cases abiding. This was the first camp-meeting in North Carolina. They soon became common all over the South and West. Log-cabins were built at the accustomed or designed place of meeting in sufficient numbers to accommodate a large assembly; and from an occasional meeting they became regular appointments, which are not yet entirely discontinued.

"The excitement spread rapidly over the congregations in the upper part of Orange Presbytery, which then included all the State east of the Yadkin river; and in the early part of 1802, the Presbytery of Concord, embracing the section of the State west of the Yadkin, and the eastern part of the State, now embraced by Fayetteville Presbytery, began to be visited.

"In all our charges were families who had been principally engaged in promoting and holding religious societies, and were engaged in fervent prayer for a time of refreshing from the presence of the Lord; some of them for more than eighteen months before that time. And should this little narrative be thought worthy of the public eye, my design in it is to encourage God's children to be fervent at the throne of grace, not only in secret, but social prayer. From what I have known of the fervency and persevering importunity of those families upon whom that remarkable effusion of divine grace fell, I think I never saw a geometrical proposition demonstrated with more clear evidence than I have seen an answer given to the prayers of those pious parents.

"At all our meetings a considerable number professed to obtain the comforts of religion, and, of those, I have not heard of one whose conduct has dishonored his or her profession. Praying societies are formed in all our congregations, both supplied and vacant. In those the work seems to be promoted as much, and often more than in our congregational assemblies. The face of the public, in point of morals, is evidently changed for the better, even in those places where the good work has not reached. It is to me no inconsiderable proof that the work is carried on by the same Divine, omnipresent Spirit, when I behold such a sameness of exercises in the different subjects."

The labors of the Rev. James Hall, who was Moderator of the General Assembly in 1803, were greatly blessed.

His preaching was "clear, earnest and pungent." In a letter to the *New York Missionary Magazine* he narrated some of the circumstances of several "general meetings held in the Presbytery of Concord." At one of these, fourteen Presbyterian ministers were present, and eleven of other denominations. He says, "This was by much the most numerous and solemn assembly I ever beheld. There were within the camp three places for public preaching, and all occupied by vastly large assemblies. The number present on that day could not be less than six or seven thousand."

It is worthy of remark that some in these great crowds of people came from great distances, in midwinter, and that the exercises in the open air were uninterrupted, though the days were "the most inclement of the winter." On a Saturday morning a violent storm of rain fell upon the worshipers, which "turned to sleet, succeeded by a mixture of snow, and this followed again by rain," and yet such was the intense anxiety to hear the words of eternal life, that the multitude around the different speakers "continued there until within half an hour of sunsetting, when we requested them to retire to their tents to take some refreshment, promising that we would there wait upon them in the night."

Many of the ministers from South Carolina, Georgia and Virginia, hearing the amazing tidings of the revival in Kentucky, Tennessee and North Carolina, visited those States to satisfy themselves as to their genuineness, and returned to start the flame of them among their own people. The *Rev. James McGready* writes:

"By the latest accounts we hear that the flame has reached *South Carolina*, and is going on with rapid progress. I would just mention, for the comfort of God's people in your country, that I never knew a revival with fewer instances of deceptions or delusive hopes. It is truly astonishing to find those who are delivered from their burden of guilt and distress to be the subjects of such clear, rational, scriptural views of the gospel scheme of salvation, and the nature of Christ's satisfaction to the law and justice, and his willingness to save guilty, lost sinners. It is a common case for illiterate negroes and little children of five, six, seven and eight years old, when they get their first comforts, to speak of their views of the mediatorial glories of Christ; his fullness, suitableness and sufficiency to save to the uttermost; their views of the holiness of God and the purity of the divine law, and such like subjects, with an eloquence and pathos that would not disgrace a preacher of the gospel."

In Rev. Dr. Foote's *Sketches of Virginia* it is said:

"The excitement, with some of its peculiarities, was felt in *Virginia*, first in the Presbyterian settlements along the head-waters of the Kanawha, in Greenbrier County. Here were no stated ministers. Missionaries occasionally visited them. The work began at a prayer-meeting of private Christians. Ministers from Kentucky recognized here the power of spiritual truths over the minds of men, as they had seen it in the West.

"In the latter part of the year 1801, the churches under the care of Messrs. Mitchel and Turner were greatly revived. A meeting held at the close of the year was noted for the number of people impressed with a deep sense of the value as well as truth of the gospel. Many made profession of their faith. In the succeeding spring the influence of Divine truth was felt with increased force. The Presbytery of Hanover met at Bethel. Crowds attended upon the ministrations of the gospel. About one hundred had now professed conversion. The congregations in Albemarle, in Prince Edward and Charlotte, were greatly awakened, and the happy influence was felt over a large region of country east of the Blue Ridge.

"The awakening continued in different parts of the Synod for some years. There were many hopeful converts where there was no stated ministry or regular church organization. Many of these, looking in vain to the Presbyterian Church for the living ministry, turned their attention to other denominations prepared to supply their wants, and are now lost to the Presbyterian Church. The demand for educated ministers came pressing on the Synod. She looked to her colleges and to the sons of the Church and to her God for the supply."

CHAPTER VI.

GREAT RAINS OF GRACE IN THE EASTERN STATES.

THE Holy Spirit descended in smaller measure upon many places in the Middle States east of the mountains, and along the Northern Lakes, at the same time in which the rains of which we have been speaking came down so copiously throughout the West and South.

The preaching of Dr. Alexander McWhorter of Newark, *New Jersey*, the Moderator of the General Assembly in 1794, was always powerful and affecting. Numerous revivals were granted to his church. But in 1802 there was one of extraordinary extent and continuance—one hundred and forty persons were brought in during two years, under the pastoral labors of his successor, Dr. E. D. Griffin. Previous to it Dr. Griffin was in much distress. He says: "As I was walking in the streets of Newark, pondering upon my sins, a flash of light came across my mind, sending home a conviction of sin which instantly deprived me of hope. The following dialogue then took place with myself: 'Well, go to Christ as you direct others to do.' 'But he is away beyond the hills, and I cannot get to him.' 'Well, ask him to bring you to him.' 'But the prayers of the unregenerate cannot ascend above the clouds. I have nothing to stand upon to begin.' I felt then totally undone, helpless and hopeless. I did then as Paul did on the plains of Damascus. Instantly the scene changed. I was composed in a moment, and seemed to lie down at God's feet and rest every issue on his will without a struggle." Then he learned, as he says, to leave it at last to Christ, and his preaching became "full of Christ." (*Stearns: History of the First Church, Newark.*)

The eminent Robert Finley, named by Dr. Archibald Alexander "the father of the American Colonization Society" (*History of African Colonization*), was "an able, evangelical and uncommonly successful preacher." It is narrated (*Sprague: Annals*) that at Baskenridge, in 1803, "a revival of great power took place among his people at the same time that other churches in the neighborhood were visited in a similar manner. The number admitted to the communion as the fruits of this revival was about one hundred and fifty."

The devoted laborers, Henry Kollock, James Richards, and others, went forth among the destitute mountain regions of Northern New Jersey, "especially to the iron mines and furnaces." "The tears flowed down the cheeks of the hardy men" there under the power of the truth. There were revivals in other parts of the State. Four years later the former blessings were renewed in some of these places, under the preaching of the celebrated Dr. Gideon Blackburn, of Tennessee. Dr. Griffin said of it, "The work, in point of stillness and power, exceeds all I have ever seen."

The State of *New York* during the last century was gradually colonized westward by a bold and enterprising class of people, some of whom, like the same class in the new States of the West to-day, were speculators in land, or those whose misfortunes, or vices, or roving character, disposed to regard with distaste the staid associations and habits of older communities, and to cast off the obligations of religion. It was long a common saying, "Religion has not got west of the Genesee River." Some of the towns were hotbeds of infidelity; and the books of Tom Paine, Voltaire, and their tribe, were largely circulated through the country.

In the eastern part of the State the labors of the godly Seth Williston, whose name must ever be dear to many through some of his writings, of Jedediah Bushnell, and other faithful men, were the means of the conversion of large numbers. The winter of 1798 was marked "by a wonderful display of divine power and grace in the conversion of sinners" in Palmyra, Canandaigua and several of the larger towns along the southern border of the State. But the most memorable outpourings of the Holy Spirit were later. "The year 1800, for a long period," says Dr. E. H. Gillett, in his *History of the Presbyterian Church*, "was destined to be remembered throughout the region as the year of The Great Revival." "It commenced at Palmyra, and soon extended to Bristol, Bloomfield, Canandaigua, Richmond and Lima, and to other places in a less marked manner." "The doctrines," said Williston, "which God makes use of to awaken and convert sinners are those which are commonly distinguished as 'Calvinistic.'" The Rev. James H. Hotchkin (*History of Western New York*) says of the revival of 1799–1800:

"The counties of Delaware and Otsego were powerfully

affected by it. So also was the county of Oneida, which lay to the north. It was a general shaking of the valley of dry bones. God manifested himself in his glory in building up Zion. The tide of infidelity, which was setting in with so strong a current, was rolled back, and Western New York was delivered from the moral desolation which threatened it. The general prosperity, the religious order, the benevolent and literary institutions, which constitute the glory and happiness of this section of country, it cannot be doubted, are in no inconsiderable degree attributable to the change produced in the current of public sentiment, as the consequence of this extended revival of religion. The year 1798 is an era which should long be remembered in Western New York, as giving a character to this part of the State which laid a foundation for its large prosperity and improvement in all things useful."

Amidst the sober population of *New England* the fruits of the previous labors of many able and godly servants of Christ appeared in numerous places. In some congregations, in which since the times of Jonathan Edwards there had been little or no evidence of the special presence of the Spirit of God, there were sudden effusions of extraordinary power. Then, indeed, said Dr. *Porter*, subsequently professor at Andover, "the day dawned which was to succeed a night of more than sixty years. As in the valley of Ezekiel's vision, there was a great shaking. Dry bones, animated by the breath of the Almighty, stood up newborn believers. The children of Zion beheld with overflowing hearts, and with thankful hearts acknowledged, 'this is the finger of God.' The work was stamped conspicuously with the impress of its Divine author, and its joyful effects evinced no other than the agency of Omnipotence." This was at Washington, Connecticut. At numerous places in Connecticut and Massachusetts there were, as the Rev. *Moses Hallock* said, displays of Divine powers and grace which far exceeded what they "ever before saw." "The revival," remarks Dr. *Shepperd,* of Lenox, Mass.," began in the church, as I believe is almost always the case when God pours out his Spirit." "The work has been attended with remarkable regularity. God was emphatically in 'the still small voice.' No dreams and visions, no hearing unusual voices and seeing uncommon sights, no extravagance even in gestures or outcries, appeared. The power of the Holy Spirit was not controlled by ordinary rules, nor did it operate according to the expectations of men. Some who had long sat under the teachings of the house of God were left to hardness and impenitence; and others were pierced with extraordinary views of the truths of God's word or of nature." "One instance, somewhat singular, may be worthy of note. There was a respectable man who remained an attentive observer till near the close of the awakening, without any particular operation on his own mind. Going one day out of town, on a law suit, it turned in his mind that the Bible was the best law book, the eternal rule of right between man and man. The same thought occurred to his mind frequently when going home, and when he retired for the night; but it gave him no particular alarm. When he awoke before day the same impression was running in his mind, 'The Bible is the best law book.' He rose, made a fire, and while he sat meditating upon this impression, all at once his soul was filled with rapture, and ere he was aware, he was 'like the chariots of Amminadib.' He beheld such glory and beauty in the Divine character as he could not describe, and his mouth was immediately filled with praise. He set up family duties, and continued in this sweet and comfortable frame of mind for a considerable time without thinking of its being a change of heart; but finding his soul filled with love to God, drawn forth with peculiar affection towards the brethren, and the most earnest desire for the salvation of souls and a delight in the duties of religion, he was led to hope he had become a new man, and was admitted to the church, where he has adorned his profession."

The Great Revival reached out into the wildernesses of Vermont and New Hampshire, and some of their hardy inhabitants became bright trophies of the power of redeeming grace. In no part of the country were the best fruits of it more abundant than in New England; not alone in souls converted, but also in the organization of evangelistic and charitable institutions which have proved a blessing to the nation and to the world.

CHAPTER VII.

TESTIMONIES AS TO THE GENERAL CHARACTER OF THE REVIVAL OF 1800.

IT will give us more confidence in the character and fruits of this vast and mighty work to notice the judgments which were formed of it at the time by capable witnesses, omitting reference to the excesses or peculiarities which appeared about its course in some regions.

The Rev. Dr. *Heman Humphrey*, long President of Amherst College, who was in the Freshman class at Yale in 1802 when the college was visited with such a revival as it had never before known, says in his *Revival Sketches:*

"In looking back fifty years and more, the great revival of that period strikes me, in its thoroughness, in its depth, in its freedom from animal, unhealthy excitement, and its far-reaching influence on subsequent revivals, as having been decidedly in advance of any that had preceded it. It was the opening of a new revival epoch which has lasted now more than half a century, with but short and partial interruptions—and blessed be the God, the end is not yet.

"Thus the glorious cause of religion and philanthropy has advanced till it would require a space which cannot be afforded in these sketches, so much as to name the Christian and humane societies which have sprung up all over the land within the last forty years. Exactly how much we at home and the world abroad are indebted for these organizations, so rich in blessing, to the revivals of 1800, it is impossible to say, though much every way—more than enough to magnify the grace of God in the instruments he employed, in the immediate fruits of their labors, and the subsequent harvests springing from the good seed which was sown by the men whom God delighted thus to honor. It cannot be denied that modern missions sprung out of these revivals. The immediate connection between them, as cause and effect, was remarkably clear in the organization of the first societies which have since accomplished so much; and the impulse which they gave to the churches to extend the blessings which they were diffusing, by forming the later affiliated societies of like aims and character, is scarcely less obvious. Taken altogether, the revival period at the close of the last century and the beginning of the present furnishes ample materials for a long and glorious chapter in the History of Redemption."

The Rev. Dr. *Gardiner Spring*, the venerable pastor of the Brick Church, New York, was a convert in another revival in the same institution the next year. He thus writes (*Personal Reminiscences*):

"From the year 1800 down to the year 1825, there was an uninterrupted series of these celestial visitations spreading over different parts of the land. During the whole of these twenty-five years there was not a month in which we could not point to some village, some city, some seminary of learning, and say, 'Behold what God hath wrought!'

"I marvel not a little, that, after all our eyes have seen and our ears have heard, there should be good men among us who look with suspicion upon these days of mercy, and who do not rather hail them, even in this midnight of our national tribulations, as the harbinger of that predicted period 'when the light of the moon shall be as the light of the sun, and the light of the sun shall be seven-fold, as the light of seven days.' This is a ruined world; I should give up all for lost, unless God thus appear in his glory, and build up Zion. There is no other helper, there is no other hope!"

The Rev. Dr. *Samuel Ralston*, of Allegheny County, Pennsylvania, a laborer amidst the harvest scenes, in his *Letters* showing, in opposition to certain enemies of the work, that it was "agreeable to the Word of God," and kindred with the great revivals in Scotland and in New England, testifies that "this work was begun and carried on in this country under the preaching and influence of the doctrines contained in the Confession of Faith of the Presbyterian Churches." "That this work is a gracious work of the Spirit of God is apparent to me from the effects it has produced. It has reclaimed the wicked and the profligate, and transformed the lion into a lamb. It has brought professed deists to become professed Christians, and turned their cursings into blessings and their blasphemies into praises. Many who could not relish any religious conversation are now only delighted when talking about the plan of salvation and the wonders of redeeming love; and many, very many, give evidence by their life and conversation that they are born of God. And to this I would add, that it has had this effect on many of all ranks, ages, sexes and colors; the African as well as the European and American. The combined hordes of deists, hypocrites and formalists are generally opposed to it. Some also have fallen away, but this is no objection, but rather an evidence that it is the work of the Spirit of God."

The Rev. Dr. *Moses Hoge*, of Virginia, when he had witnessed and had an opportunity to judge of some of these outpourings in 1802, in North Carolina, wrote to Dr. Ashbel Green, of Philadelphia, "This work seems to lead to a more clear and distinct view of the operations of the Divine Spirit upon the heart of a sinner in his conversion and in subsequent communications than can be obtained from ordinary revivals. For, as a pious and sensible woman of this country has well expressed it, Jesus Christ seems to be there, exercising in a visible manner his offices as a Mediator."

The Rev. Dr. *George A. Baxter,* of Washington Academy, Virginia, visited Kentucky in 1801, and thus describes his conclusions as to the Revival in that section of the country, in a letter to Dr. Archibald Alexander:

"I left the country about the 1st of November, at which time this revival, in connection with the one on the Cumberland, had covered the whole State of Kentucky, excepting a small settlement which borders on the water of Green River, in which no Presbyterian ministers are settled, and I believe very few of any denomination. The power with which this revival has spread, and its influence in moralizing the people, are difficult for you to conceive, and more so for me to describe. I had heard many accounts, and seen many letters respecting it, before I went into that country; but my expectations, though greatly raised, were much below the reality of the work. Their congregations, when engaged in worship, presented scenes of solemnity superior to what I had ever seen before. And in private houses it was no uncommon thing to hear parents relate to strangers the wonderful things which God had done in their neighborhoods, while a large family of young people, collected around them, would be in tears. On my way to Kentucky, I was informed by settlers on the road that the character of Kentucky travelers was entirely changed, and that they were now as remarkable for sobriety as they had formerly been for dissoluteness and immorality. And indeed I found Kentucky, to appearance, the most moral place I had ever seen. A profane expression was hardly ever heard. A religious awe seemed to pervade the country. And some deistical characters had confessed that, from whatever cause the revival might proceed, it made the people better. Its influence was not less visible in promoting a friendly temper among the people. Nothing could appear more amicable than that undissembled benevolence which governs the subjects of this work." "As an eye-witness in the case, I may be permitted to declare that the professions of those under religious convictions were generally marked with such a degree of engagedness and feeling as willful hypocrisy could hardly assume." "Upon the whole, I think the revival of Kentucky among the most extraordinary that have ever visited the Church of Christ." "Extraordinary power is the leading characteristic of this revival. Both saints and sinners have more striking discoveries of the realities of another world than I have ever known on any other occasion."

For the sake of its precious lessons we will quote the testimony of one more witness from the many who might be brought forward. The Rev. *David Rice* preached a sermon at the opening of the Synod of Kentucky, in 1803, in relation to the general beneficent character of the Revival in that section of our country. His interesting and impressive words should be deeply considered by those who desire a return of the Holy Spirit to our churches now, and are willing to use the means which a sovereign God has appointed to secure so unspeakably great and precious a favor from Him.

1. "This revival has made its appearance in various places, without any extraordinary means to produce it. The preaching, the singing, the praying, have been the same to which people had been long accustomed, and under which they had hardened to a great degree; and the first symptoms of the revival have been a praying spirit in the few pious people found among us. They somehow got their minds impressed with a sense of their own backsliding; with a sense of the prevalence of vice, infidelity and impiety; and an unusual compassionate concern for the salvation of precious souls who were perishing in their sins, and for the prosperity of Zion. They prayed; they endeavored to excite their friends and neighbors to pray; they formed themselves into praying societies, that they might mutually encourage and assist each other. *The revival appears to be granted in answer to prayer*, and in confirmation of that gracious truth, that God has 'not said to

the house of Jacob, seek ye me in vain,' when he says he 'will be inquired of by the house of Israel to do it for them.'

2. "As far as I can see, there appears to be in the subjects of this work a deep heart-humbling sense of the great unreasonableness, abominable nature, pernicious effects and deadly consequences of sin; and the absolute unworthiness in the sinful creature of the smallest crumb of mercy from the hand of a holy God. There appears to be in them a deep mourning on account of their own sins, the sins of their fellow professors, and the sins of the careless and profane, and particularly for the base sin of ingratitude to God for his many mercies; and conviction of the justice of God in condemning and punishing his offending creatures.

3. "They appear to have a lively and very affecting view of the infinite condescension and love of God the Father, in giving his eternal and only-begotten Son for the redemption of mankind; and of the infinite love of the Redeemer, manifested in the great and gracious work of redemption; manifested in the labors and sorrows of his life and of his death: an affecting view of the astonishing goodness of the adorable Trinity, in providing and applying a complete atonement for the sin of fallen man, and a perfect righteousness for his justification. And all this in a way that not only secures, but advances, the honors of God's law and government, and illustrates his justice, holiness, truth and tender mercies. Jesus Christ, and him crucified, appears to be the ALL IN ALL to the subjects of this revival, and the creature nothing and less than nothing.

4. "They seem to me to have a very deep and affecting

sense of the worth of precious immortal souls, ardent love to them, and an agonizing concern for their conviction, conversion and complete salvation. As far as I can judge, they are pleading for this with strong, fervent desires, with deep humility, with faith in God's promise and in the merits and intercession of Jesus Christ. Perhaps the ardency of their love sometimes hurries them into some indiscretions which excite the prejudices of those for whose salvation they are pleading. Men are imperfect creatures; and these, if I may be allowed the expression, appear to be the generous blunders of benevolence. This love, this compassion, this ardent desire, this agonizing, this fervent pleading for the salvation of sinful men and for Zion's prosperity, far exceed any thing I have ever seen. This love, these fervent supplications, are not confined to a particular spot or a particular party. They extend to and include men of every description: Catholics and Protestants, Jews, Mohammedans and Pagans. The most savage nations, who are sunk almost beneath the notice of others, are embraced in the arms of their benevolence. Little children lie near their hearts; they take them in their arms and put the hands of their benevolence upon them, and plead with the Father of mercies to bless them. O thou Fountain of mercy, give me, give to all, this spirit of love, of grace and of supplication!

5. "A considerable number of individuals appear to me to be greatly reformed in their morals. This is undoubtedly the case within the sphere of my particular acquaintance. Yea, some neighborhoods, noted for their vicious and profligate manners, are now as much noted for their piety and

good order. Drunkards, profane swearers, liars, quarrelsome persons, etc., are remarkably reformed. The songs of the drunkard are exchanged for the songs of Zion; fervent prayer succeeds in the room of profane oaths and curses; the lying tongue has learned to speak truth in the fear of God, and the contentious firebrand is converted into a lover of peace. A number of poor backsliders appear to be sensible, that 'it is an evil thing and a bitter that they have forsaken the Lord their God,' and are returning to him with penitent hearts, going and weeping, inquiring the way to Zion with their faces thitherward, and we hope are joining themselves to the Lord in a perpetual covenant never to be forgotten.

6. "A number of families, who had lived apparently without the fear of God, in folly and in vice, without any religious instruction or any proper government, are now reduced to order, and are daily joining in the worship of God, reading his word, singing his praises, and offering up their supplications to a throne of grace. Parents who formerly seemed to have little or no regard for the souls of their children are now anxiously concerned for their salvation, are pleading for them and endeavoring to lead them to Christ and train them up in the ways of piety and virtue. Masters who formerly treated their servants as brutes are now earnestly concerned for the salvation of their souls, and using means to promote it.

7. "The subjects of this work appear to be very sensible of the necessity of *Sanctification* as well as Justification, and that 'without holiness no man can see the Lord;' to be greatly desirous that they themselves and 'all that name

the name of Christ should depart from iniquity,' should recommend the religion of Jesus to the consciences and esteem of their fellow men, that the light of their holy conversation should so shine before men that they, seeing their good works, might give glory to God. A heaven of perfect purity and the full enjoyment of God appears to be the chief and ultimate object of their desire and pursuit.

"Now I have given you my reasons for concluding the *morning is come*, and that we are blessed with a real revival of the benign, the heaven-born religion of Jesus Christ, which demands our grateful acknowledgments to God the Father, Son and Holy Ghost."

The *General Assembly of the Presbyterian Church* in 1803 appointed a committee, consisting of Rev. Messrs. Samuel Miller, Archibald Alexander and James Welsh, "to draw up a statement as the result of the free conversation on the state of religion." To favorable testimonies which it had given in previous years it added the following:

"The Assembly heard at more than usual length, and with more than common satisfaction, the accounts received from their members of the state of religion within the bounds of the Presbyterian Church. Since an inquiry of this nature has become a part of the annual business of the Assembly, it may be confidently asserted that no result was ever presented to our body so favorable and so gratifying to the friends of truth and piety.

"There is scarcely a Presbytery under the care of the Assembly from which some pleasing intelligence has not been announced, and from some of them communications have been made which so illustriously display the triumphs of evangelical truth and the power of sovereign grace as cannot but fill with joy the hearts of all who love to hear of the prosperity of the Redeemer's kingdom.

"In most of the Northern and Eastern Presbyteries, revivals of religion of a more or less general nature have taken place. In these revivals the work of Divine grace has proceeded, with a few exceptions, in the usual way. Sinners have been convinced and converted by the *still small voice* of the Holy Spirit, and have been brought out of darkness into marvelous light, and from the bondage of corruption into the glorious liberty of the children of God. Many hundreds have been added to the Church in the course of the last year, and multitudes of those who had before joined themselves to the Lord have experienced times of refreshing and consolation from his presence.

"In many of the Southern and Western Presbyteries revivals more extensive and of a more extraordinary nature have taken place.

"It would be easy for the Assembly to select some very remarkable instances of the triumphs of Divine grace which were exhibited before them in the course of the very interesting narratives presented in the free conversation—instances of the most malignant opposers of vital piety being convinced and reconciled; of some learned, active and conspicuous infidels becoming the signal monuments of that grace which once they despised, and various circumstances which display the holy efficacy of the gospel. But, forbearing to enter into minute details on this subject, they would only in general declare that in the course of the last year there is reason to believe that several thousands within the bounds of the Presbyterian Church have been brought to embrace the gospel of Christ, and large accession of zeal and of strength as well as of members given to his people.

"The Assembly consider it as worthy of particular attention, that most of the accounts of revivals communicated to them stated that the institution of praying societies, or seasons of special *prayer to God* for the outpouring of the Spirit, generally preceded the remarkable displays of Divine grace with which our land has been recently favored. In most cases, preparatory to signal effusions of the Holy Spirit, the pious have been stirred up to cry fervently and importunately that God would appear to vindicate his own cause. The Assembly see in this a confirmation of the word of God, and an ample encouragement of the prayers and hopes of the pious for future and more extensive manifestations of Divine power. And they trust that the churches under their care, while they see cause of abundant thankfulness for this dispensation, will also perceive that it presents new motives to zeal and fervor in application to that throne of grace from which *every good and perfect gift cometh.*

"The Assembly also observed with great pleasure that the desire for spreading the gospel among the destitute inhabitants on our frontiers, among the blacks and among the savage tribes on our borders has been rapidly increasing during the last year in various parts of our Church. The Assembly take notice of this circumstance with the more satisfaction, as it not only affords a pleasing presage of the spread of the gospel, but also furnishes agreeable evidence of the genuineness and the benign tendency of that spirit which God has been pleased to pour out upon his people.

"On the whole, the Assembly cannot but declare with joy, and with most cordial congratulations to the churches under their care, that the state and prospects of vital religion in our country are more favorable and encouraging than at any period within the last forty years."

CHAPTER VIII.

THIS REVIVAL PART OF A WORLD-WIDE ADVANCE OF THE KINGDOM OF CHRIST.

THE sketch which has been given of the Great Revival of 1800, as related to the United States of America, would fail to make a proper impression upon the minds of Christians did I not remark that it was not simply an American movement. It was part of an immense advance of the kingdom of the Lord Jesus Christ which can be distinctly traced amidst the populations and affairs of all the important nations of mankind.

In Eastern Asia this period was one of a new interest in the intellectual and moral improvement of the native races. The three Wellesleys, Richard, Henry and Arthur (the latter afterward the famous Duke of Wellington), commenced a new era in the administration of the British East India Company. Infanticide was prohibited by law in 1802. The conscience of the European conquerors was roused by the Parliamentary investigation into the old abuses of the servants of the Company. It was not long before Lord Minto and the Marquis of Hastings were stimulated to introduce European education. The Hindoo College, the Calcutta School Society, the School Book Society, and other excellent institutions, prepared the way for the apostolic labors of British chaplains and teachers like Claudius Buchanan, David Brown and Henry Martyn, and for the eminent missionaries, Ward, Carey, Marshman, Cran, Gordon, Lee and others like them.

China, then embraced within the influences of the same European monopolies, shared in the sympathies, and in a limited degree, especially among the colonists in the Indian Archipelago, in the missionary efforts, of the period. The Bible was translated, though imperfectly, into Chinese by Lassar and Marshman in India, and by Dr. Robert Morrison, the pioneer Protestant missionary to China proper, who went to Canton by way of America in 1807.

"The isles" of ancient prophecy, Java, Sumatra, Borneo, and others of the Indian Archipelago, were brought more widely and thoroughly under the influence of the Dutch than ever before; and zealous missionaries were sent to the native races, whose labors, though ignored or contemptuously spoken of by British writers, were blessed to the conversion of many of the people, and the establishment of Christian usages and schools among them. "The fifth continent," Australia, was colonized by being made a penal settlement for English convicts. Capt. Cook introduced our domestic animals and vegetables into New Zealand and other islands. Thus these vast regions were prepared to see "upon the tops of the mountains" the glorious light of Christianity.

The Turkish Empire, already shaken by successive wars with Venice, Hungary, Russia and Austria, was further humbled by those with France and England, and sunk to a position of inferiority and submission from which it has never risen. From this time is dated its adoption of the military system, the arts and the education of the Christian powers of the West.

The condition of Palestine and the Jewish race awakened efforts to restore to them the knowledge of the long-rejected Messiah. In 1809 was organized the London Society for Promoting Christianity among the Jews.

Africa was girded with new influences. The British in 1795 began to regenerate the regions about the Cape of Good Hope. In 1799, the noble Vanderkemp commenced, with his companions, his useful labors among the Kaffirs and Hottentots. In 1787, the British purchased Sierra Leone as a refuge for liberated slaves, and in a few years made it a crown colony. In 1796, the explorations of Bruce, and in 1799 those of Mungo Park, for the head-waters of the Nile, were given to the world. Egyptian lethargy and superstition were effectually shaken by the French and English invasions. The Moorish States were humbled by the wars with France, England and the United States.

South America was moved, by the contagion of civil and religious liberty in its twin continent of the North, to throw off the galling yoke of Spanish despotism and superstition, and a series of republics sprang forth which for a time aspired to be our rivals in the benefits offered to mankind.

All Europe was an arena in which ancient thrones were hurled to the ground and the priestly chains about the human intellect and conscience were violently broken and cast away. Napoleon Bonaparte, in the name of an apostle of social progress and the rights of man, swept from one extreme to the other of the continent. The first terrible outbursts of infidel triumph and pride were succeeded by an awakening of Christian Churches to reformation of abuses and to the duty of publishing the gospel to all nations. The Netherlands Missionary Society was formed in 1797, at Rotterdam; the Berlin Missionary Society in 1800. The Basle Missionary Society was reared in 1817, as a monument of the salvation of the city from the peril of a bombardment. In the first years of this century a score of prominent societies of a missionary and educational character were established in Western Europe. Men of great zeal and success, like Vanderkemp among the Kaffirs and Gutzlaff on the coast of China, were sent forth by them, or went abroad by the aid of funds furnished by British Societies. Republics were established in Northern Italy, and Rome itself was made one in 1802. The Pope's power was draggled in the dust as it had never been before. In Germany, the University of Berlin was made an institution of the first rank; the Lutheran and Reformed Churches were fused under the name of the "Evangelical Church." Monarchs themselves seemed moved by a new spirit. After the battle of Leipzic, the Protestant king of Prussia, the Greek Catholic emperor of Russia, and the Roman Catholic emperor of Austria united together in what they styled "The Holy Alliance," and called God to witness that henceforth they would only reign for the happiness of their subjects and the triumph of the Christian religion.

Great Britain was the scene of an equal onward movement in the kingdom of Immanuel. The success of the American Revolution was in reality the success of the cause of popular liberty, of the principles of Pitt and Burke, the beginning of that recognition of the political and religious rights of men of every rank and creed which has brought Great Britain to-day to the verge of democracy. That of France—a terrible rebound of society from the rule and misrule of Popery—for a time spread wild and fanatical infidelity among the middle and lower classes. But this was part of the stimulating cause of the more fervent preaching of the gospel by Rowland Hill, John Newton and many other zealous men, and of the formation of several of those great religious societies which have been the chief honor of modern Britain. Of these the British and Foreign Bible Society is the most important. "The formation of this Society," says Anderson in the *Annals of the English Bible*, "produced an effect altogether unprecedented; indeed, the mere announcement ran throughout every denomination in the kingdom, and conveyed an impulse at once the most powerful and the most extensive under which the Christians of this country had ever come." The Society originated, in 1804, in the proposition of two Welsh ministers, Thomas Charles and Joseph Hughes, to furnish Bibles, in their native tongue, to the people who spoke it, and to other races. The Baptists formed their Missionary Society in 1792. The London Society was organized in 1794; the Religious Tract Society in 1799; the Episcopal Church Missionary Society for Africa and the East in 1800. The Wesleyan foreign missions, commenced in 1769 in North America, in 1792 were extended to Sierra Leone; in 1796 to the Foullahs in Africa; in 1799 to Gibraltar; in 1800 to Madras, in India. Indeed, the Spirit of God communicated a universal interest in the condition of the degraded and vicious classes of society, and in the dark and helpless state of the heathen and Mohammedan nations, so that the whole Christian world started into efforts to translate into all languages, to circulate and to preach the word of the living God. All branches of the Christian Church were powerfully quickened. So wonderful, indeed, was the life and energy communicated to some of them that they have assumed their influence to have been that which moved the rest.*

But we must look far higher. The Great Revival of 1800 was an element in the beginning of the grandest advance of Christianity since the Reformation of Martin Luther. It was the impulse to the universal scattering abroad of the seed which had been ripening since the time of Luther,

* It is sometimes claimed by Baptists that the establishment of their Society in 1792 was the origin of the modern missionary efforts of other Churches. This is without foundation. The Rev. Dr. F. A. Cox, in his *History of the Baptist Missionary Society* (Vol. I. p. 4), though himself a Baptist, quotes one of its early addresses which declares that "it was proposed at first, if no opening was found for a Baptist mission, to have requested the Presbyterian and Moravian brethren, who had been already employed in laboring among the heathen, to accept some assistance from our subscriptions; for by the leave of the God of heaven, we were determined to do something towards propagating his gospel in heathen lands." There were missions, of long standing and considerable success, sustained by Reformed, Presbyterian, Lutheran and Moravian Churches, in numerous heathen fields, in various parts of the world.

The Great Revival, in the United States was mainly Calvinistic in its character, but it gave a powerful impulse to Methodism in some parts of the country.

Calvin and Zwingle. It was a most manifest introduction of the Divine achievement which may eternally give lustre to this *nineteenth century*—the commencement of those grand, universal and final effusions of the Holy Ghost which shall convert the whole of this lost world to God.

CHAPTER IX.

POWERFUL EFFECTS OF THE GREAT REVIVAL UPON OUR CHURCH-LIFE—ORGANIZATION OF THE SEVERAL BOARDS.

IT is most interesting to trace the influence of the Great Revival in the development of the several departments of labor and influence for good which we now denominate the Boards of the Presbyterian Church.

First let us look at "Home Missions." The first thought of an awakened soul is to do what Jesus commanded the demoniac out of whom he cast the legion of devils: "Go home to thy friends, and tell them how great things the Lord hath done for thee, and hath had compassion on thee." It is most worthy of observation that ministers were powerfully attracted even from other and distant States to the scenes of the great outpourings of the Holy Spirit. Thence they returned, publishing as they went the glad tidings, and starting other communities to pray for the same wondrous gifts of mercy. "As when the melting fire burneth, the fire causeth the waters to boil, to make Thy name known to Thine adversaries, that the nations may tremble at Thy presence." Some of the letters written by the ministry thus engaged narrate their manifold labors, and mention the exhaustion of their physical strength by incessant preaching and conversation with the impenitent and inquirers. The General Assembly had long maintained systematic efforts "towards supplying the destitute portions of our country with the preaching of the gospel." But at this time the duty took a more enlarged and efficient form. The Rev. Dr. Green (*Historical Sketch of Domestic and Foreign Missions in the Presbyterian Church*) says, "In 1802 an important alteration took place in the manner of conducting the missionary business. It had now become so extensive" as to require "a Standing Committee of Missions to act throughout the year," "clothed with such powers as were then deemed sufficient." This committee made, in 1803, its First Annual Report "to the General Assembly." The series thus instituted has been continued till this time. The Standing Committee on Missions was increased in the number of its members and in its powers in 1816, and the name changed to "The Board of Missions." The late New School branch of the Church, which had carried on its Home Mission operations through the agency of the American Home Missionary Society (another of the fruits of this great movement), established, in 1847, its own work under the designation of "The Standing Committee on Home Missions." "The Board of Home Missions" of our reunited Presbyterian Church is therefore a great and precious monument of that outpouring of God's Spirit which compelled the formation of a permanent organization, in behalf of the General Assembly, to care for the multitude of destitute flocks, to send the gospel to the frontiers, and to be the agency through which the Church should do her part toward filling the whole land with the means of grace through the preaching of the word.

Our cause of "Foreign Missions" is also directly connected with the Great Revival of 1800. The deepest pity is excited, in the breasts of those who know the joy of deliverance from the bondage of hell, for those fellow immortals who sit in the deepest darkness, and who are most helpless beneath the ancient fetters of Satanic dominion. It is wonderful to mark the instant reaching forth of tender sympathy, in that Revival, toward the poor Indian tribes. There are no people whose desolate wretchedness—plundered as they are, slaughtered, crushed by the weight of vices which often white men have taught them, and poisoned by diseases which white men have communicated—more profoundly excites Christian sorrow and commiseration, and to whom the Church, when warmed afresh by the Spirit of the merciful Redeemer, more anxiously desires to convey the balm of peace through his atoning blood. The Presbyterian Church has for more than a century carried on missionary operations with more system, continuousness and zeal than any other. In 1741 the Presbytery of New York sent forth Azariah Horton, and in 1744 David Brainerd, supported by the "Society in Scotland for Propagating Christian Knowledge," to preach to the Indians in New Jersey and Eastern Pennsylvania, and in 1776, Charles Beatty and George Duffield to preach to those upon the Muskingum river in Ohio.

The revival period about 1800 gave new life to such missions. The New York Missionary Society was formed in 1796, chiefly through the efforts of the Rev. Dr. John M.

Mason, one of the great preachers of the age. It looked beyond our continent, and across the Pacific. In an Annual Report, under Dr. Mason's signature as Corresponding Secretary, in 1803, it speaks of the breaches now made "in the once undisturbed strongholds of Satan," and says, "a little more, and irruptions will be made in his securer possessions, not perhaps to be resisted till the light of the glorious gospel of Christ shall beam on the waters of the Pacific ocean, and his blessed name shall resound from her shores." He hoped some of the converted Indians might be the means of carrying "westward into Asia the light of life and immortality." He little dreamed that, when the Chinese would be brought by God to seek here that light, many of our own people would try to drive them back to darkness again. The Synod of Pittsburg, at its first meeting, upon its organization by the act of the General Assembly, in September, 1802, solemnly resolved the body itself into a society to be styled "The Western Missionary Society," whose object was "to diffuse the knowledge of the gospel among the inhabitants of the new settlements, the Indian tribes, and, if need be, among some of the interior inhabitants where they are not able to support the gospel." There was constituted at the same time a "Board of Trust," consisting of seven members, to manage the missionary concerns of the Synod. This was the beginning of the series of missionary efforts which terminated in the organization of the "Board of Foreign Missions" by the General Assembly of 1837, which transferred the work begun in Pittsburg to the city of New York. The Secretary of the Western Foreign Missionary Society, the Hon. Walter Lowrie, who had formerly been a Senator of the United States from the State of Pennsylvania, and was elected Secretary of the new Board, was one of the converts of the Great Revival. Through a long and laborious life he infused the fervor of that Revival into all his correspondence, toils and influence, and made its power felt in the Presbyterian foreign missions which sprang up in every continent.

We may next observe how the Great Revival was related to "Ministerial Education."

A powerful outpouring of the Holy Ghost upon a community or land necessarily compels many of the men converted to leave their nets and their seats at the receipt of customs, and follow in the footsteps and labors of their Master. It compels those who cannot go forth to preach, to feel that a closely related duty to our perishing race lies upon them, and cannot be avoided—that is, that if they cannot *go*, they must *send* others in their place. Thus its era is commemorated by permanent monuments in the form of collegiate and theological institutions, and by the establishment of ecclesiastical organizations to multiply and educate candidates for the ministry.

The revival of 1730–50 was the means in God's hands of rousing the Presbyterian Church to feel the necessity of a college in the Middle States. Hence the origin of that at Princeton in 1746. Its great object was, as the Synod of New York in 1754 informed the General Assembly of the Church of Scotland, to endeavor to make "provisions for many shepherdless flocks," and for those "that come hundreds of miles crying to them for some to break the bread of life among them, and are often obliged to return in tears with little or no relief by reason of the scarcity of ministers." "And were the poor Indian savages sensible of their own case, they would join in the cry, and beg for more missionaries to be sent to propagate the religion of Jesus among them."

The Great Revival of 1800 created an immense demand for ministers. The Synod of Virginia in 1798 enlarged Liberty Hall into Washington Academy. In Kentucky and Tennessee the rising interest gave existence to Washington College in the year 1796, and when a few years later scores of new congregations demanded pastors, which could not be at once supplied, it led, in the end, to the introduction of uneducated and incapable men into the pulpit, and to the painful schism of the "Cumberland Presbyterian Church" from the parent body. In Western Pennsylvania it begat Jefferson and Washington Colleges, only a few miles apart, and somewhat later, Allegheny College; and in New York, in 1796, Union College, which has always been essentially Presbyterian, and in 1812, Hamilton College.* But the most marked advance in Ministerial Education was the determination of the General Assembly in 1810, after much discussion for some years previously as to the form and number of such institutions required, to erect a Theological Seminary, and it was carefully announced "that, as filling the Church with a learned and able ministry, without a corresponding portion of real piety, would be a curse to the world and an offence to God and

* In Ohio, Miami University, at Oxford, was established in 1803, Ohio University, at Athens, in 1802, each aided by public grants of land, but Presbyterian in their origin.

his people," the Seminary should endeavor "to train up persons for the ministry who shall be lovers as well as defenders of the truth as it is in Jesus, friends of revivals of religion, and a blessing to the Church of God." The institution in the year 1812 was located at Princeton, N. J.

One of the incitements to the establishment of the Princeton Seminary was the success of that in a sister Presbyterian body which had been conceived by Dr. John M. Mason, in 1796, and put in operation in 1805. The latter was the model also of the earliest Congregational Seminary at Andover, Mass. (*Memoirs of Dr. Mason.*)

It was but a short time until other seminaries, to train the young men pressing toward the ministry and needed for the fields everywhere ripe for the sickle, sprung up in other portions of the country. Auburn, for Central and Western New York; the Western Seminary, for the large Presbyterian population of which Pittsburg is the centre; Columbia, for the Synods of South Carolina and Georgia; Lane, for the region centring at Cincinnati; Union Seminary, for the Synods of Virginia and North Carolina; Danville, for Kentucky and the country south of it; the Indiana Seminary, which after various transmutations has found a permanent home at Chicago; and the New York Union Seminary,—all, with some others not aiming so high, were planted successively within the seventeen years beginning with 1818.

The increase of candidates for the ministry all over the land compelled the adoption of a general system to collect money to aid them and to superintend the cause of Education.

In 1806, the Assembly, as it was said, in view of the obvious and melancholy fact that the candidates for the gospel ministry within the bounds of the Presbyterian Church at present fall very far short of the demand made for their services, "adopted a plan for the general and harmonious action of the Presbyteries in the employment of certain means to increase their number, raise funds for their support, and inspect their education. This plan was followed until 1819, when the Assembly established a "General Board of Education." The principles of this Board are essentially those which the Church has matured in the present form, which was adopted at the reunion two years ago, enriched with the suggestions of the experience of each of the bodies.

In the formation of this Board those who twenty years afterwards parted into the two temporary branches of the Church were cordially agreed. The godly and zealous Drs. James Richards, William Hill, James P. Wilson, E. S. Ely and Rev. James Patterson, all of them men eminently blessed in their labors, worked to accomplish it with the faithful and scholarly Drs. Ashbel Green, Archibald Alexander, Samuel Miller, J. J. Janeway, William Neill and Rev. Francis Herron.

This more complete shape was a result of the secondary revival impulse which about that period brought into action the American Bible Society, the American Tract Society, the American Board of Commissioners for Foreign Missions, the American Colonization Society, the American Education Society, and other beneficent institutions.

While the Great Revival of 1800 created a demand for

ministers, and excited the Church to organize means to increase the number of them, it completed what was necessary to supply them, by mightily affecting the young people of the land. It led a great number of young men into the ministry. It wrought wonders in some of the few academies and colleges then in existence. At Princeton its blessed influences were missed through the dispersion of the students by a fire which burned the college building. The youth of the institutions in the West and South were bathed with its powerful influences. The ministers in those regions labored with special zeal for the conversion of the young. And they pressed into the ministry and made provisions to educate, for the supply of the gospel to the multitudes awakened by the Great Revival, the most fervent and capable of the young men who were brought by it into the Church. The Rev. Dr. McMillan alone, according to *Dr. Matthew Brown*, of Jefferson College, was the instrument of fitting for the ministry, in his academy, one hundred men, many of whom were eminently useful. Speaking of the fellow-laborers of McMillan, the *Rev. Dr. Gillett* (*History of the Presbyterian Church*) says: "Rarely, if ever, in the history of the Presbyterian Church in this country has any of its missionary fields been occupied by a more able and devoted band of pioneer laborers than that which was covered by the Old Redstone Presbytery. Many of them were rarely gifted, and would have done honor to the most exalted station; and the influence which they exerted upon the great Western field, then opening with inviting promise to Eastern emigration, cannot be estimated. They wanted, and made provision to secure, *strong* men, and all who joined them seemed to be made partakers of their spirit." Dr. *H. Humphrey* thus describes the effects of this wonderful work of grace at Yale College: In "the spring and summer of 1802 the revival, in its triumphant progress on the right hand and the left, reached Yale College; and there it came with such power as had never been witnessed within those walls before. It was in the Freshman year of my own class. It was like a mighty rushing wind. The whole college was shaken. It seemed for a time as if the whole mass of the students would press into the kingdom. It was the Lord's doing, and marvelous in all eyes. Oh what a blessed change! As the fruit of this revival, so memorable in the history of the institution, fifty-eight were added to the college church, and others, I know not how many, joined the churches at home. It was a glorious reformation. It put a new face upon the college. It sent a thrill of joy and thanksgiving far and wide into the hearts of its friends who had been praying that the waters of salvation might be poured into the fountain from which so many streams were annually sent out. The triennial catalogue shows that for many years there had been but very few in the seminary preparing for the pulpit. In the four preceding classes, only thirteen names of ministers stand against sixty-nine in the next four years—nearly, if not quite, all of them brought in by the Great Revival."

Such must be the logical effects of a genuine revival of religion. Such they have been in the past—such they must be now. Only the Holy Spirit can constrain parents to give their sons to go they know not where, preaching the gospel to mankind, or to take of the substance which they are laying up for their heirs, and give it to educate the sons of strangers for that end. No motives but those with which the Holy Spirit moves the souls of men can draw gifted and energetic young men from the overwhelming attractions which the world has to offer, and lead them heartily to consecrate themselves to the comparatively toilsome, ill-paid and anxious office of the ministry. He alone can inspire them with patience and diligence in the tedious prosecution of long years of needful preparatory study. And only a general pervading influence of the Spirit of God can enlist the membership of the Church in the proper support of a department of her work which has so little that is exciting or romantic in its details, to catch the imagination, and to stimulate pecuniary contributions. Thus it is that the cause of Ministerial Education is one of the first to feel the influences of a genuine outpouring of the Holy Spirit; and these influences it soon sends streaming, in an energized generation of ministers, through every branch and fibre of the Church's outward life.

The principles of the work of our "Board of Publication" began to receive practical application during the Great Revival.

A Jewish funeral, in a time of war with the heathen Moab, carried out a dead man. Surprised by a band of enemies, they cast the body into the tomb of a prophet by whom God had long before wrought many mighty miracles. When the corpse touched the bones of Elisha he revived and stood upon his feet!

Centuries ago, Augustine, Calvin, Luther, were laid in their tombs. Edwards, Baxter, Bunyan, have gone to dust. But the mysterious seed of spiritual life remains, and ever will remain, in the books which they have left. Millions of dead souls have touched them, and straightway revived and stood upon their feet.

Religious books had been purchased from time to time by the General Assembly from its funds for the use of the poor. But with the Great Revival this duty puts on a form and activity of which we see little trace in its previous history. In 1801 and '2, when reports are poured in of extensive regions nearly or "wholly destitute of the means of religious instruction," the Assembly resolves that "religious books should be sent for gratuitous distribution along the frontiers of these States, among the poorer classes of people, to the blacks, or wherever it may be thought useful; which books shall be given away, or lent, at the discretion of the distributor." Within a few years, the need of more system in the publication and distribution of religious books and tracts, and the collection of funds for the gratuitous part of the work, led Dr. A. Alexander and others to organize what was possibly "the primitive Tract Society;" and the celebrated physician, Dr. Benjamin Rush, in 1808, took the lead there in planting the "Philadelphia Bible Society," "the oldest in the hemisphere." (*Life of Dr. A. Alexander.*)

The want of books, and the anxiety of the people to hear of the wonderful tidings of the spread and power of the gospel, produced several monthly religious magazines, such as "The New York Missionary Magazine," "The Connecticut Missionary Magazine," "The Christian Remembrancer," at Philadelphia, and "The Western Missionary Magazine," at Washington, Penna., whence are drawn most of the precious narratives of God's doings at this period. These led the way to our Church periodicals.

The present form of the Board of Publication is the combination, since the reunion, of the organs which were established by the two branches of the Church subsequent to their separation—the Board in 1838, the Permanent Committee in 1852. The body of Presbyterian literature which it circulates, through its colporteurs, over all the land, is a perpetual refreshment of the faith and zeal of the Church by the teachings of the living and the record of what our fathers have believed and wrought through God; thus its work is a great preparation of the Church, and of tens of thousands without her pale, for the more glorious days which are coming.

The general organizations under the care of the General Assembly, the "Board of Church Erection," and the "Committee on Freedmen," are branches of work formerly included within the sphere of Home or Domestic Missions, but which, from their great importance and the distinctness of their objects, have now been appointed to separate representative commissions. The "Relief Fund for Disabled Ministers and the Widows and Orphans of Deceased Ministers" is a newer outgrowth of our evangelistic spirit. The more active and widespread a war, the greater necessity for hospitals and provision for the disabled soldiers and those who suffer through them.

A general survey of the Revival of 1800 leaves the impression that, beyond the purpose of mercy to that generation, there may be traced in it a special design of the almighty Head of the Church; that is, the *organization of Protestantism* for the evangelistic efforts of this age. We have seen this in Great Britain, Germany, Holland and the United States. The history of our Presbyterian Church in this country, which we have been considering, remarkably illustrates it.

CHAPTER X.

THE SIGNS OF A NEW ORDER OF HUMAN AFFAIRS.

WE have taken a rapid glance at the Great Revival epoch in which the Church of Christ was lifted, with the beginning of the nineteenth century, to a much higher plane of spiritual life and energy.

We would not attach a vital importance to the regularity of the cycles in which the history of redemption often runs. But an inspired writer has thought fit to introduce the life of Jesus Christ with the observation that "all the generations from Abraham to David are fourteen generations, and from David until the carrying away into Babylon are fourteen generations, and from the carrying away into Babylon unto Christ are fourteen generations."

It pleased God to stamp seven as a symbolic number upon many ordinances, divisions of time, and multiples of things which are more or less related to the sanctifying and peace-giving operations of the Holy Spirit. He appointed seventy as the definite and significant number of the judges of his people; of the years of their chastisement for disloyalty to their Sabbath duties; of the subsequent weeks of years until the Messiah should come; and of the messengers next the apostles in rank whom he sent to proclaim the gospel of peace. We simply do not understand in this terrestrial state what this spiritual astronomy means. It is too high for us. But we may notice that there is a similar periodicity in the grand revivals of modern Christianity, dating from Luther at Leipzic and the Diet of Worms, in 1519 to 1521. The close of the century witnessed the prosperity of Protestantism in France under the Huguenot king, Henry IV., and the first colonization of this New World by Sir Walter Raleigh. Then we have, in the series, the triumphs of spiritual religion under the protectorates of the Cromwells, ending in 1660; the "Great Awakening" of 1730; and the Great Revival of 1800. We seem to have reached another of these eras. We behold another act of the testimony to alternate generations. We appear to be entering upon another and higher and swifter stage of the career of the gospel of salvation.

But in the cycles of the Sun of Righteousness, and at least the earthly system which revolves about him, there is another and far grander significance to be imputed to the period in which we live. It is one of the most ancient and firm beliefs of large sections of the human race, Christian, Jewish and Mohammedan, indications of which may be traced even among heathen nations, that, as a thousand years with the Lord is as one day, so the history of the world is marked by the sabbatic seal upon its greatest cycles, that each thousand years is a day, the week of which will be terminated by a glorious "rest," a "millennium" of holiness and peace, an earthly "sabbatism" which will breathe its spirit over the entire race of man, and bring the world into a new and closer intercourse with God and heaven. It has been the expectation that the later generations of the present thousand years would behold the grand preparations and renovations which would introduce that happy period.

Could the twelve apostles of the Lord Jesus be summoned back, as were the great lawgiver and the great prophet, to the scene of the manifestation of the glory of their Master, and lifted to take a general survey of the preparation of the nations of the world for the gospel at this time, they would see that it finds nothing equal to it since their own wonderful and culminating era. The empire of Japan, abolishing the ancient idolatry of Buddhism by law and bursting forth into a mighty entreating cry for intellectual and spiritual light; China, queen among nations, hoary, humiliated, bruised with blows and draggled behind the chariot of rude and avaricious foreign conquerors, ready to yield any demand to save her life, and throwing open the gates of a thousand cities to the preachers of a new and dreaded doctrine; India, revolutionized since the terrible Sepoy rebellion, penetrated with five thousand miles of railroad, her deified Ganges compelled to scatter its waters to irrigate and give life to once barren wastes, the revenues of her temples forfeited, hundreds of thousands of her sons rejecting the decrepit wisdom and the complicated creeds of their fathers; the shah and court of Persia putting off beard and turban and robes, wearing European dress and conforming to Western ideas; Egypt spanned by railroads; Ethiopia explored by Christian missionaries; miracles of salvation wrought in Madagascar; Russia rising through the peaceful and voluntary emancipation of her serfs; Spain, Austria, Italy and France breaking the heavy chains of a thousand years of despotic papal rule, and admitting freedom of conscience and of public worship, with all the liberalizing influences of Protestantism in their train; slavery abolished in America; civilization and the gospel reaching the "going down of the sun" on its Western shores, and the commingling there of the ancient races of the East with ours; the globe netted over with railroads and telegraphs and lines of steamers; the tens of millions of books; the hundreds of millions of newspapers; the Bible translated into every important language; Christian hospitals, Christian schools, Christian printing presses, Christian commercial and literary and social influences penetrating and leavening all heathen, Mohammedan and anti-Christian lands. Above all, the prophecies of God's word fulfilled in the destruction of the temporal power of the Roman anti-Christ; the hopeless abasement of the Mohammedan false prophet; and the supremacy of the nations which were the seat of the Great Reformation three centuries ago, in positions whence they may control the future destinies of mankind. We seem to be fairly merging into the full sunrise of a new order of human affairs. The state of the world reminds us of that when it advanced from the planetary and prophetic but unsatisfying light of Judaism into the cloudy twilight of the past two thousand years. Now the clear sunlight begins to dawn over the hills. What Christianity truly is, and what it can do to bless mankind, now begins fully to appear before all the world.

It seems to be in accordance with truth for us to assert that in the condition of mankind there has never been anything to compare with what now exists since that "fullness of times" when Jesus came to make atonement. Then he came as Priest. Now he manifestly prepares to come as King. The Father was glorified then by his obedience to the law. The Father shall be glorified now by the success of the word which he gave, and in that the disciples bear much fruit. The Spirit was manifested then in a ministration of forms. The Spirit is to be manifested now in a ministration of glory; he leads the sons of God into all truth; he lavishes upon them the fullness and riches of his heavenly gifts. Such is the resemblance, and the contrast, of the beginning and the end of the present order of things in the kingdom of God.

Thus we are irresistibly led to overlook all the intermediate advances and lapses of Christianity, and to connect the glorious promise of its beginning with the prophecies of what it shall be when it fairly girds up its loins and starts upon its unrestrained career. The past revivals have been but the troubled movements, the inarticulate sighs, of a Church which now wakes up and puts on her beautiful garments, and prepares, with all her queenly train, to meet her Lord.

The interpreters of God's word point to many signs of the approach of "the latter days." "Many run to and fro," the world is traversed by multitudes as it never was before, who crowd the means of universal communication; "and knowledge is increased," multiplied, popularized, cheapened, and given to the poor and the laboring classes by numerous forms of the publication of it, and by national and other systems and methods of education of the young.

There do "come in the last days scoffers walking after their own lusts." The prophetic term of the papal superstition seems to have expired. The Waldensian witnesses have come down from their wilderness, and again lifted up their testimony. The angels of chastisement go forth again in wars, conflagrations, pestilences, famines. The gospel of the kingdom is preached to all the world. By such signs this seems to be linked peculiarly with the apostolic era of Christianity.

If this general sentiment of Christians, and indeed of mankind, be correct, then the Church of Jesus Christ is called to rouse herself to put on the spirit and meet the duties of the occasion. And especially is she required to go to the inspired account of the beginning of the course of the gospel; to study the teachings, character, toils, events, of that period of mighty evangelic success; and to pray and labor with the expectation that all its wonders will be tenfold multiplied in the world-wide closing scenes of this Dispensation, preparatory to a holier and happier state of the world.

CHAPTER XI.

THE LATTER PENTECOST.

THE climate of Palestine supplies one of the most plain and apposite illustrations of the method of the operations of the Holy Spirit. After a long and torrid summer, in which no rain falls from the unclouded sky, and vegetation is lifeless through the extreme and unbroken heat, as in our Atlantic regions in the winter from the opposite cause, about November "the former rains" set in. For some weeks, *through the seed time*, there are plentiful and reviving showers. All nature puts on fresh beauty. Flowers, grasses and the whole vegetable world start with new life. But after a time the periodic supply seems to be effected, and the rains almost cease. For two or three months there descend but light and temporary showers. But when spring sets fairly in, and nature feels a further general necessity, when the swelling seed of a thousand hills and valleys needs new and bountiful gifts of moisture to enable it to fill, and multiply, and enrich the earth with the final and useful products, then the heavens are again opened; then descends the copious "latter rain;" it is the grand *preparation for the harvest.*

"Ask ye of the LORD rain in the time of the latter rain; so the LORD shall make bright clouds, and give them showers of rain, to every one grass in the field." The prophet Zechariah takes the wonderful illustration from the laws of the descent of rain in that climate, and uses it to tell *us*, in "the latter day," our duty. Dr. E. Henderson (*Commentary on the Minor Prophets*) thus translates the verse:

> "Ask ye from Jehovah rain in the time of the latter rain:
> Jehovah maketh the lightnings,
> And giveth them the heavy rain,
> To every one grass in the field."

Zechariah is the Isaiah of "the minor prophets;" full of the most evangelical, distinct and far-reaching predictions. In a passage in the ninth and tenth chapters we read first the cry: "Rejoice greatly, O daughter of Zion; shout, O daughter of Jerusalem: behold thy King cometh unto thee; he is just and having salvation; lowly, and riding upon an ass, and upon a colt the foal of an ass. . . . He shall speak peace unto the heathen; and his dominion shall be from sea to sea, and from the river to the ends of the earth." A little farther on is the promise before quoted.

This most striking prophecy is kindred with a group found in both the Old and New Testaments, which declare that there shall be a great outpouring of the Holy Spirit, glorifying the third person of the Trinity by an overwhelming manifestation of his attributes at the close of this Dispensation, and before the millennium; just as the second person of the Trinity was glorified by a manifestation of himself at the close of the last Dispensation, and as the introduction to this one. The passage depicts the period of this Divine manifestation; the reviving influence of it upon the world; the tempestuous and startling judgments which shall be sent upon the nations, the lightnings which shall precede and accompany the rains; and the great abundance of the converts, which is often in Scripture compared to that of the blades of grass in the fields. On the other hand, man's part, in the use of the ordained means, is made prominent and essential: the Church *must* "*ask*" for these wondrous gifts. In a similar prediction in the book of Ezekiel it is written: "Thus saith the Lord God, I will yet for this be inquired of by the house of Israel, to do it for them; I will increase them with men like a flock."

And it is a matter of the very first importance that we shall study, ponder, pray over, this declaration of the eternal and omnipotent God until we are deeply convinced and affected with the sense that they relate to *us*, that they point to *our* age, that they define *our* duty. God, by his Holy Spirit, will give unto us, if asked, this deep and realizing conviction. This will be to us the spring of confidence, of exertion, of patience, of supplication and of joy.

The word "*ask*" is not, in the Hebrew, simply to request. It is the reverential supplication of the queen of Sheba when she *asked* counsel and instruction of King Solomon; the passionate entreaty of Hannah when she *asked* a son from the Lord; the anxious prayer of Solomon when he *asked* wisdom as the highest gift God could bestow upon a youthful sovereign; the *begging* of a person for bread to keep him from perishing, or the supreme duty which God *requires* of man. Our duty is to ask, to pray, to beg. Let us inquire how the primitive Christians prayed, to receive such amazing gifts as those of Pentecost.

The *first* impression which we receive from the study of the closing scenes of the life of Jesus Christ, and that of the spirit of the disciples, is that they were *intensely affected with the dreadful and desperate state of men without Christ.*

Jesus' tears over Jerusalem had moved their inmost soul. "If thou hadst known, even thou, at least in this thy day, the things which belong to thy peace! but now they are hid from thine eyes. For the days shall come upon thee that thine enemies shall cast a trench about thee, and compass thee round, and keep thee in on every side, and shall lay thee even with the ground, and thy children within thee; and they shall not leave in thee one stone upon another; because thou knowest not the time of thy visitation." It is probably beyond our power to conceive of the passionate love of the Jew for Jerusalem, the seat of ten thousand wondrous records and legends of God's favors to his race, from Abraham's day till Christ's; of saintly characters which were to those of the rest of the world what a planet is to an earthen lamp; of amazing national deliverances by Divine and by angelic hands; of promised glory to Israel by the incarnation, in their stock, of the Son of God; of a looked-for kingdom which should surpass any earthly dominion by as much as God is greater, mightier, wiser, richer, than man. *Now*, with the terrific denunciations of Jesus upon the people, the awful woes which hung over the city and land, so painfully described, as to their fulfillment, by Josephus—the fatal hemming in by the implacable Roman hosts, the eating of their own babes in the extremities of famine, the ferocious feuds and bloodshed within the walls, the rivers of blood poured down the declivities and into the brooks when the city was taken, the burning and complete destruction of the city and temple, the pitiless sweeping away of all classes and ranks into distant and hopeless slavery—all before the eyes, the ears, the imaginations, the hearts, of these fervent preachers of salvation, who can realize the anguish of their prayers for themselves, their kindred and their countrymen? Who can feel as they did the crushing force of that damning charge, the murder of their own MESSIAH, which they hurled at the people of Jerusalem? "HIM ye have taken, and by wicked hands have crucified and slain." "Ye denied the HOLY ONE AND THE JUST, and desired a murderer to be granted unto you; and killed the PRINCE OF LIFE, whom God hath raised from the dead."

A look of Jesus sent the conscience-stricken Peter out to "weep bitterly." What must have been the bitterness of the weeping, the agony of the acknowledgments, the intensity of the entreaties for mercy upon those who had "pierced him," which filled that upper chamber during the days which intervened between the distressing scene when the disciples stood "gazing up into heaven" after their departed Lord, and that when the Holy Ghost was given in fulfillment of his last promise, and they were clothed with unknown power as preachers of the new doctrines!

To conceive and to feel something of the present and the eternal woes of those who reject the Son of God, who "pierce him," who "crucify him afresh," to pray with genuine sincerity of desire and entreaty for their deliverance and pardon,—this is the first step towards our moving Jesus to send down the gifts of the first Pentecost. We can scarcely hope for "the heavy rains" of the time of the "latter rain" until Christians are affected to pray for the pardon of their own guilt, and for the rescue from eternal damnation of their ungodly kindred, their unconverted fellow-citizens, and the countless millions of the world lying in sin, with somewhat of the depth of emotion and urgency of supplication which at the first Pentecost so mightily moved the heart of God, and opened so wide the windows of heaven.

It was the deep conviction of these things which gave power to the preaching of the Great Revival of 1800. The reader of this account of it must have felt it in the words which the preachers have left on record; and their daily labors "from house to house," like the primitive Christians, were in the same spirit. The Rev. Samuel Andrews (*Historical Collections*) says of Rev. S. C. Caldwell, of North Carolina, "He pungently presented the truths of the gospel and delineated the character of saints and sinners with close application to every man's conscience, and before he dismissed the congregation he besought them again to attend to the things which belonged to their everlasting peace. While he spoke the tears frequently rolled down his cheeks. He also exhorted families and conversed with individuals about their eternal interests."

The *second* strong impression which we receive from a study of the scenes at and after Pentecost is, *the adoring honor, the implicit faith, the joyful love of those Christians toward Jesus Christ.* "They worshiped him, and were continually in the temple praising and blessing God." Study this wonderful picture: "They lifted up their voice with one accord, and said, 'Lord, Thou art God, which hast made heaven and earth and the sea and all that in them is. Of a truth, against Thy holy child Jesus, whom Thou hast anointed, both Herod and Pontius Pilate and the people of Israel were gathered together, for to do whatever Thy hand and Thy counsel determined before to be done. And now, Lord, behold their threatenings, and grant unto Thy servants that with all boldness they may speak Thy word, by stretching out Thy hand to heal, and that signs and wonders may be done by the name of Thy holy child Jesus.' And when they had prayed, the place was shaken where they were assembled together, and they were all filled with the Holy Ghost."

What a linking together, in their faith, of the divinity of Jesus with all its attributes and the humanity with all its sympathies! What reliance on Him who was made a little lower than the angels, for the suffering of death, that he might lead many sons into glory, but is now crowned with all glory and honor, and all things put in subjection under him!

"Adoring angels round him fall,
  In all their shining forms;
His sovereign eye looks through them all,
  And pities mortal worms."

"JESUS" was the great theme of their talk, their thoughts, their preaching, their joy! "With great power gave the apostles witness of the resurrection of JESUS, and great grace was upon them all." "Daily in the temple, and in every house, they ceased not to teach and to preach JESUS CHRIST," and "rejoiced that they were counted worthy to suffer shame for his name." "And the Lord added daily to the Church such as should be saved."

The theme of the great day of wonders, the special Pentecost, was, "Repent and be baptized, every one of you, in the name of JESUS CHRIST, for the remission of sins, and ye shall receive the gift of the HOLY GHOST. Save yourselves from this untoward generation." "And the same day there were added unto them about three thousand souls."

O brethren, this is the power that "shakes the place" where we assemble for prayer; that shakes the strongest fortification which human pride or hatred, or Satan's power, can rear about the souls of men; that can shake the whole world with fear and into submission!

When Justin Martyr was summoned before the Roman prefect and asked what was the creed of himself and his associates, he replied, "That we should worship the GOD of the Christians, whom we believe to have been from the beginning One, the Creator and Maker of all things, even of all things seen and unseen, and the LORD JESUS CHRIST who was predicted by the prophets as the future Saviour of mankind." When Polycarp was condemned to be burned at the stake, he cried, "O true and faithful GOD, I bless Thee! I glorify Thee, with the eternal and heavenly JESUS CHRIST, Thy beloved Son, to whom, with Thee and the HOLY SPIRIT, be glory now and for ever." This faith was the power that overwhelmed the Roman empire, that converted millions over the whole world.

It was the name of JESUS that shook all the world at the Great Reformation. "In my heart," said Martin Luther, "this article reigns alone, and shall reign, namely, *faith in my dear* LORD CHRIST, who is the only Beginning, Middle and End of all my spiritual and divine thoughts which I have by day or night." And again: "Ah, how truly grand is the honest prayer of a true Christian! How mighty it is with God, that a poor human creature can so speak with the High Majesty in heaven, and not dread Him, but know that God is kindly smiling on him, for JESUS CHRIST'S sake, His dear Son, our Lord and Saviour!" This was also the spirit of Zwingle and Calvin.

Would we again shake the world, it must be by the power of JESUS CHRIST; by preaching JESUS CHRIST, his complete and finished atonement, his all-sufficient intercession, the efficacy of his word, the honor of his kingdom on earth, the joys of his kingdom on high; and by praying to JESUS CHRIST that he would send the HOLY SPIRIT to convince all the world of sin, of righteousness and of judgment, according to the eternal covenants of mercy.

Where shall we *find help? Not* from any arm of flesh. Among the African races, as indeed among most of the heathen, there is a class of "rain-doctors" who, in a protracted drought, are employed to excite the heavens and bring down the precious showers. They erect a stage and make incantations, howlings, drummings, hideous contortions. They burn clouds of incense and offer sacrifices. And they and their followers believe that their efforts possess some efficacy. Just such there were among the heathen nations about Palestine. The Scriptures often allude to them. But who alone can send rain? "Let us now fear the LORD our God that giveth rain, both the former and the latter, in his season." How are we to obtain it from God? Not by our own efforts. Not by the juggling of professional revivalists. "*Ask of the* LORD rain, in the time of the latter rain, so the Lord shall send lightnings and give them [heavy] showers of rain, to every one grass in the field." "Elijah was a man subject to like passions as we are, and he prayed earnestly that it might not rain, and it rained not on the earth by the space of three years and six months. And he prayed again, and the heaven gave rain, and the earth brought forth her fruit."

Prayer is the only power that can rend the heavens! Secret prayer—with a shut closet door, to him who has covenanted to reward us openly. Family prayer—"every family apart, and their wives apart," as Zechariah instructs us; and how God is waking up our wives and sisters and daughters to pray now, as if an earnest of his blessing! General prayer—that "the land shall mourn;" prayer in the house of God, prayer in our presbyteries, synods and assemblies, conventions of ministers and of elders for prayer, general days of fasting and prayer, weeks of prayer.

Will not the LORD JESUS, the same almighty Head of the body, the Church, who is before all things, and by whom all things consist, answer sincere, believing prayer? —He who says reproachfully to us, "hitherto ye have asked nothing in my name; ask and ye shall receive, that your joy may be full—that the Father may be glorified in the Son." Once the disciples were in peril, their ship seemed about to sink with the roaring and dashing waves.

And they came to him, and awoke him, saying, Lord, save us, we perish! And he saith unto them, Why are ye fearful, O ye of little faith? Then he arose, and rebuked the winds and the sea, and there was a great calm. And the men marveled, saying, What manner of man is this, that even the winds and the sea obey him! Let *us*, fellow disciples, set ourselves to *wake him.* The winds, the clouds, shall obey him!

A *third* leading feature of the Pentecostal epoch was that the converts seemed so *wholly filled with the temper and spirit which might be expected to possess "children of God."*

When we read the history of a great sovereign we expect to find that his virtues have been transmitted by nature, by his precepts and by his illustrious example, to his sons and daughters. We are greatly disappointed if we learn that the family of such a king were self-indulgent, sensual, cowardly, avaricious, and that their conduct dimmed the glory of their paternal name.

In the revelations which God has made of himself in his word we learn of the infinite excellence of all his moral attributes. It is in accordance with reason to expect that when he adopts "children" they shall catch from his word and by the promised influences of his Holy Spirit upon the soul such goodness, benevolence, purity, justice and other heavenly traits as shall make them shine in this world of sin like a different order of beings, almost as it were angels in disguise.

Such were the first converts of Christianity. They were all sinful by nature and imperfect; some of them fell into gross offences. But if any one will endeavor to picture to his mind a man moving among ourselves possessed of the virtues of one of those primitive Christians best known to us—for instance, Paul—his love, patience, generosity, courage, devotion to his Master's work, elevation above the motives and spirit of the people around us with whom we are acquainted,—we will realize something of how greatly they differed from us. Few, it is true, equaled him. But still in him we see much of the prevailing character of the first disciples of Christ.

Let us select one high characteristic of those men and women. There is no sin which should more clearly distinguish the world from the church than the love of money. Jesus Christ thus marked it: "Ye cannot serve God and mammon." The apostles held up its dangerous, subtle, mighty power over the soul and over the conduct in such warnings as this: "The love of money is the root of all evil." It is a sin which cuts the cords of dependence on our Father's providence; the ties of association with heaven and its inhabitants, and superiority to the world; and the strong obligations of generosity and hospitality to our brethren in Christ, and of gospel liberality in publishing the knowledge of salvation to all the world.

How were the first converts in respect to this sin? It is remarkable that the inspired historian, in the Acts, at once proceeds from the description of the outpouring of the Holy Ghost upon the day of Pentecost to say: "And all that believed were together and had all things common, and sold their possessions and goods, and parted them to all men as every man had need. And they continued daily with one accord in the temple, and breaking bread from house to house, did eat their meat with gladness and singleness of heart, praising God and having favor with all the people. And the Lord added daily to the church such as should be saved." And the narrative of another Divine effusion very soon afterwards says at once: "Neither was there any among them that lacked; for as many as were possessors of houses or lands sold them, and brought the prices of the things that were sold, and laid them down at the apostles' feet; and distribution was made unto every man according as he had need." Then we read the good example of the liberality of Barnabas, and the bad one of the covetousness of Ananias and Sapphira, and their destruction, *first* for covetousness, then for lying.

Now, if *money* be, as it is, the equivalent, the representative, the means of *power*—the stimulus, present compensation and support of all forms of mechanical, commercial and other material and intellectual employments for the ends to which they are directed—it is seen in a moment *why* its consecrated use is a supreme duty; and *why* its abuse, by wasting it, by consuming it upon our appetites, or by laying it up in a napkin, and burying it in land or investments, where it cannot germinate in good, is a sin which stands near that which is unpardonable.

When heathen, who are accustomed to large outlays for religious purposes, and do not dream that they "cannot give" for such objects, are converted—when they take their tone, not from us American and European Christians, but from the word of God, its teaching and its examples—their liberality seems to the people of our day extravagant.

Thus I have seen poor converts bring in loads of fruit, vegetables and articles of their own manufacture, on a missionary occasion. A ministerial brother in China mentioned the case of a man, who earned about six dollars in a month, that usually managed to bring savings to the amount of one dollar, to help to send the word of God to his perishing fellow-countrymen. The sons and daughters of affliction are at times chastened to something like the primitive liberality. A poor blind girl once brought to her pastor several dollars in money. He expressed his surprise. She replied that she had saved it by laying away as much money as persons who see would have spent for candles. Thus her sorrow and darkness were lighted with the light of the smiles of her Saviour. Our little children, too, how their simple faith in God, their readiness to give freely and thankfully the money or the other treasures which they possess, when their hearts are touched with some narrative of woe, humbles our spiritual self-satisfaction, and rebukes our oversight of that model which our Master placed before us! "Jesus called a little child, and set him in the midst of them, and said, Verily I say unto you, except ye be converted, and become as little children, ye shall not enter into the kingdom of heaven." Millions of professing Christians probably have discovered the truth of this declaration when, dying amidst mourning families, who had enjoyed with them the abundance of the things of this life, they found to their eternal horror the gates of the kingdom of heaven *shut*. They had called themselves "children of God;" he says, "I never knew you."

But "with what measure" do we mete? Look at the

contributions of many a congregation in a substantial farming community. The annual aggregate of the gifts of some churches for the spread of the gospel over our nation or abroad, or to educate men for the ministry, or for the increase of religious literature, or to any of the other great avenues of evangelization which God has opened before us, may be as much as the price of an ox, or a sheep, which any one of a hundred members might give away, or lose, and be none the poorer. Indeed, many give, to save their fellow-men, nothing at all. Look at those from churches in cities or towns—a yearly consecration to some work of Christ, from the whole body, of what one of many members would spend for an evening's entertainment and mirth.

When we consider the torpor of the Church to this and other sins of omission as well as transgression, we may well ask, Is it a wonder that God's Spirit is withheld? That our children grow up unblessed? That dissipation and folly prevail in society? That scoffers deride the precious name of Christ? That tens of thousands of thinking and moral people stand aloof from the Church? That the wheels of the chariot of salvation are clogged? That the world is trenched in its superstition and unbelief? We must warn men to repent of the *robbery of God*, and bring the offerings which they owe, before he can "open the windows of heaven and pour us out a blessing."

What a power the American Church would have for the spread of the gospel if its members employed the vast, varied, inexhaustible resources of this wonderful continent in the service of Christ, as they do to maintain armies and navies and the fleets of commerce, to carry railroads to the extremes of civilization, to multiply manufactures, to increase the products of the soil, to rear edifices for the multifarious uses and desires of our luxurious and extravagant state of society, to get riches that "bereave the soul of good," and that are kept for children "to their hurt"!

Was there ever an age in which such opportunities and means were given to the Church of Christ to reach and benefit and bless mankind? Was there ever a generation so guilty as ours in closing its eyes and ears to the despair of the perishing immortal beings around us? Was there ever one to whom, by all the grand vehicles of a high civilization, their woes, their ruin, their terrors, their blind helplessness while they are falling over the precipices of eternal perdition, were so brought before the eyes, the ears, the imagination? Oh, did we consecrate thought, time, property, sons and daughters, all the numerous and potent influences of our day and land, to publishing that joyful, wonderful, glorious news, with anything like the same devotedness to him which glowed in the first Christians, how quickly all our continent, all Asia, all Africa, all Europe, would be filled with the praises of his redemption!

When we compare the *three* great revivals of American history, we may observe a progression in their character.

The *first* was one of *colonization.* It made the dead formalism of Europe intolerable, and placed a renovated and free people upon a new, unoccupied and suitable continent. This was the digging up and the transfer of the ore.

The *second* was one of "*awakening,*" as it was well termed at the time. It was one of doctrinal instruction, of spiritual quickening; and it is wonderful how the holy influence of Jonathan Edwards, David Brainerd and others of that day is to be traced at the root of the revival and missionary efforts of all sects and lands. This was the melting and fining of the metal.

The *third* was one of evangelic *organization.* It girded and arrayed the followers of Christ, some of them in general societies, some of them in the establishment of separate ecclesiastical agencies, for the great work of giving the gospel to mankind. I have shown how the Boards of the Presbyterian Church can be traced back to it. This was the advancement to the building of engines and machinery.

The *fourth* must be one of *dissemination.* It must employ the numerous membership and the vast resources of the Church in conveying the knowledge of salvation "to every creature." This must supply fuel, kindle the fires, man and load the trains and vessels, and send the freights of mercy over land and sea, to every inhabitant of this land, and to every mortal and immortal descendant of those who were driven from Eden for their sin. "*They shall obtain joy and gladness, and sorrow and sighing shall flee away.*"

Now again, "*the kingdom of heaven is at hand!*" Shall we mumble over our phylacteries, cleanse our cups and platters, and garnish the tombs of dead prophets? Shall we hold our peace? Or shall we haste with our best gifts to the KING; wake our sons and daughters to proclaim his approach; and sound the glad tidings to the meek, the broken-hearted, the captives? Is the PRESBYTERIAN CHURCH—are *we*—"*come to the kingdom for such a time as this*"? Or shall God destroy us, and raise up *help from another quarter*"?

www.ingramcontent.com/pod-product-compliance
Lightning Source LLC
LaVergne TN
LVHW021427110826
845150LV00007B/2126

* 9 7 8 1 4 2 5 5 0 7 7 2 5 *